This Book Belongs To

_____

Stay Living Intentionally To
Transform & Thrive
In Life

A Kingdom of God
Royal Family Kommunity

Copyright

Embrace Your Royalty: Learn God's Truths, Grow As His Royal Family

Table Of Contents

For more information, you can contact Monica Renee' at:

- **Email: staylittministries@gmail.com**
- **Social Media:**
  - **TikTok @choosingthekingdom**
  - **Instagram: @Staylittllc**

Monica is an Educator & Optimizer. She has dedicated her life to Transforming Education, Improving Information, Enhancing Emotional Wellness and Cultivating Discipleship and building Kingdom Kommunities through speaking, teaching, writing, mentoring, Safe Sircle Book Journeys, hosting retreats, convening Safe Sircle Social events and Stay LITT Ministries. Her work fosters spiritual growth, a Kingdom mindset, and the adoption of Kingdom identity, culture and lifestyle. Through her teaching, speaking and small groups, she encourages practical application of God's Word to transform lives from the inside out, empowering individuals to live the royal lifestyle in truth, love, wellness, joy, divine identity and in alignment with God's word and purpose.

Monica actively inspires and equips others to live with truth, joy, faith, purpose, wellness and intentionality, creating safe spaces for believers to grow spiritually in their relationships with God, cultivate life giving relationships, heal, share their faith, and practically apply God's Word to make a transformative impact in their lives and the world.

Forward

With immense joy and gratitude, I write this foreword for *"Embrace Your Royalty: Learn God's Truths, Grow As His Royal Family."* This book is more than a devotional; it is a transformative journey that invites families to embrace their royal identity in Christ and live out Kingdom values.

Monica, a cherished sister and protégé, attended the Leading Lights Training and Experience in Chicago a few years ago. Witnessing her transformation through the training was a profound blessing. Her dedication and growth led her to join our facilitation team, where she has continued to shine brightly, embodying the principles of Kingdom living.

Monica shared that this book was partly inspired by her family's use of my devotional *"365 Days In Christ—Knowing and Living Your Transformed Identity in Christ."* This devotional time catalyzed deeper understanding and living out their identity in Christ, and she felt the necessity of creating this book for families. Seeing how this seed has grown into the rich and impactful journey presented in this book is heartening.

"Embrace Your Royalty" is designed to guide families through a 30-day intentional journey into Kingdom culture. The journey focuses on values such as love, humility, wisdom, and gratitude. Each day offers a practical approach to living out these values, fostering spiritual growth and unity within the family.

Monica's heart for God and her passion for helping others embrace their divine identity are evident throughout this book. It is a testament to the power of discipleship, devotion, and God's transformative grace.

As you embark on this journey, I am confident that you will experience profound spiritual growth and a deeper connection with God's truth.

May this book be a beacon of light and inspiration for families everywhere. As you delve into these pages, may you discover the richness of your royal identity in Christ and be empowered to live as His royal family, reflecting His Kingdom values in all you do.

With gratitude and blessings,

Gregory Lan Ijiwola, Ph.D.

Lead Pastor, CityLight International Assembly, Chicago
CEO, Life Development Center,
Founder, The Leading Lights Global Network

Acknowledgements

First and foremost, I am sharing my deepest love, gratitude and thankfulness to Yahweh, God Almighty, My creator, Designer, Lover of my soul, Adonia, Jehovah Jireh, My source, My strength, My Daddy.   He has blessed me with this mission and his spirit is leading and guiding me throughout this journey of faith, following, growing, listening and doing a new thing, the thing he told me to do... Your word, wisdom, Kingdom, grace and love are the foundation of this work, the Kingdom Journey Guides, and my transformation, the renewing of my mind, my new identity and my work to help others to see you properly, learn you accurately, gain their divine identity in Christ and live a joyful abundant life of purpose that reflects your Kingdom values and represent you righteously in all we do, think and say as your beloved children, your royal family.

To my beloved, Merciful Gift of God, My son, Myles Nathan... Thank you so much for supporting me, encouraging me, and adding to this work with your input, suggestions, edits and being so understanding during this new journey of working, writing and following as God leads me. Your love, support and words to keep asking God along the way and to keep writing have been such a blessing as I grow and walk in faith. You are my blessing, my greatest gift from God.

To my Dad, Ernest M. Griffin, Thank you so much for your encouragement, prayers and numerous conversations that allowed me to share what God was revealing, sharing and teaching me throughout this journey. You have been such a great support and encouragement as I stepped into new waters, grew in intimacy with God, gained my divine identity and followed God in faith. Thank you Dad for being there throughout this amazing journey.

Thank you Tracie Leah for being a great support and understanding sister as we both diligently sought God and began to truly grow spiritually, in knowledge & faith and level up in our intimacy with God, experiencing God and understanding divine connections as we matured and stepped into a new path and leading by his Holy Spirit. Thank you Gustave and Renee Tucker for investing in my life and for being a safe space and catalyst of healing, transforming and seeing myself and life differently. Thank you Dr. Gregory Lan Ijiwola, for teaching me profound truths according to the Word of God, my Universal Purpose and supporting me in the process of discovering and unearthing my gifts, passions, core values and my individual purpose through the Life Development Center's Leading Lights Training Experience. Thank you all for being a support to me as I continue to grow spiritually, partnering with God and deploying my purpose to fulfill my God given mission to share his love, be a light and salt to advance the Kingdom of God.

Thank you, with a deep heartfelt appreciation, goes to all who were a part of this journey, who played an intricate role in bringing this book to life. Thank you Nina Addison, my Coach, Mentor and Praying Motivating Encouraging Sister in Christ. Thank You Shawn Robinson, my Creative Book Cover Designer. Thank You Dr. Vanesa Scott-Thompson, my dynamic editor.

**Embrace Your Royalty: Learn God's Truths, Grow As His Royal Family
A 30-Day Intentional Journey Into Kingdom Culture**

~Introduction, Purpose and Overview~

Embrace Your Royalty is a 30-Day Intentional Family Journey of Learning, Growing, Fellowship and Living Kingdom Values and Virtues as God's Royal Family.

The Guide for the Journey: Know the intention, path and plan for the journey before we begin (where we're going before we begin

Welcome to a transformative journey where we, as families—adults, children, tweens, and teens—embark on an exploration of the profound truths and principles that lay foundational knowledge and understanding of the Kingdom of God. This devotional bible study is designed to unite us in a shared purpose: to delve deeper into the Word of God, discovering the treasures, keys for living, rights, ways, promises, and privileges that await all of God's children. Together, we will lay a foundation of understanding, based on Scripture, that will guide us in living out our royal identity as children and citizens of God's Kingdom.

For the Family Devotional Journey:

Our time together in God's Word is more than a routine; it's an adventure into understanding Kingdom ways and our place in His grand design. Today, we set the path and purpose for our family devotion and bible study time, focusing on two pivotal Scriptures: Ephesians 2:19 and Matthew 6:33 (Passion Translation). These verses will serve as our foundation as members of God's Kingdom, illuminating our identity as God's chosen family. These verses share Kingdom principles that help guide us in how we live our lives as members of God's royal family.

Our time of devotion will focus our mind and heart on values and virtues of the Kingdom of God. The values and virtues that will be introduced, discussed and revisited during this family journey, include Provision, Forgiveness, Gratitude, Wisdom, Love, Humility and Unity. These virtues guide us in learning what God values(seeds) and the culture of his family, his chosen people, his Kingdom. These virtues are some of the behaviors that reflect God's values and the culture of his Kingdom. They express our moral standards as God's royal family. The values and virtues shared are the foundation of our Royalty. They lead and guide us in embracing our identity as sons and daughters of God's Royal Family. We embrace what we learn and use them to align our thinking, guide us in how we interact and treat others as well as when we make decisions.

These Kingdom values and virtues will be introduced and discussed so we can learn and plant these foundational values(seeds) of God's family, his Kingdom culture, in our hearts and minds. As we learn, we are challenging ourselves to intentionally think about them, talk about them, recognize them and practice these virtues within our family and with others. The purpose is to cultivate these values and virtues in our hearts, to guide us in how we live our lives as we grow and embrace the culture of God's Royal Family.

The virtues will be introduced, discussed and revisited to water the seeds of these values and virtues in our mind and heart, to learn God's truth, to meditate on what God values, to embrace God's truth, and apply these values in our lives to grow in our royal culture as God's Royal Family. Each time a virtue is revisited, it's a time to reflect on the last time there was an opportunity to use it. It's a time to connect as a family and share about new experiences both positive and challenging. These conversations could include sharing and discussing things seen, heard or situations you or others are currently facing. When a virtue is revisited in the journey, it is a time to share with one another and grow in our understanding of the virtue, especially recognizing the virtue, and understanding when and how to demonstrate these virtuous behaviors in different situations we face. Each time we revisit a virtue, we are intentionally increasing our learning, growing and cultivating our moral standards as God's royal family. Each day of our journey gives us another opportunity to meditate on these virtues, discuss these truths as a family and apply these values in our lives as we live and interact within our family and with others.

Discovering Our Royal Identity:

Ephesians 2:19

"So then you are no longer strangers and foreigners, but you are fellow citizens with the saints, and are of God's household." (NASB)

"So now you non-Jews are not visitors or strangers. Now you are citizens together with God's holy people. You belong to God's family." (ICB)

Ephesians 2:19 reveals a profound truth about our identity as believers in Christ. We are not outsiders or strangers; we are citizens of God's Kingdom and members of His Family. This realization invites us to see ourselves through God's eyes—as heirs of God and co-heirs with Christ, a royal identity that transforms our daily living.

Kingdom Principles to Live By:

Matthew 6:33

"But seek first His kingdom and His righteousness, and all these things will be added to you. (NASB)

"The thing you should want most is God's kingdom and doing what God wants. Then all these other things you need will be given to you." (ICB)

"So above all, constantly seek God's kingdom and his righteousness, then all these less important things will be given to you abundantly. (TPT)

Matthew 6:33 urges us to prioritize seeking God's Kingdom and His righteousness above all else. This principle challenges us to align every aspect of our lives with the values and standards of God's Kingdom, promising that as we do so, everything we need will be provided.

Purpose and Foundation:

Our journey together is rooted in the desire to fully grasp what it means to live as members of God's royal family. Each day, we will explore Kingdom virtues and discuss how our understanding of God's Word can transform our minds, influence our choices, and impact our world. We embark on this journey not as individuals but as a family united in purpose. We are seeking to grow in our relationship with the Father, to know Jesus the King more intimately, and to understand the role of His Holy Spirit in guiding us, teaching us and helping us toward living a life of abundance, freedom, and fulfillment. Our journey will start by introducing and exploring Kingdom values, virtues and scriptures. Each virtue will be revisited to cultivate these values and the Kingdom's culture. This devoted time is a special time that we use to come together as a family, to hear each other, learn from each other, support each other and be strengthened in the way we live as God's virtuous royal family, growing in our royalty.

A Kingdom-Focused Family Devotional Bible Study:

As we dive into truth through scriptures and reflect on its application in our lives, we invite each family member to engage actively. Let's support one another in discovering how aligning specific aspects of our lives with Kingdom principles can lead to transformative growth and blessings. The Days were not designed to be completed in 30 consecutive days. Let each day cover an amount of time to embrace the value, revisit it in conversations during the week and practice living it. This is a progressive journey for transformation, from the inside out. Consistency in gathering to discuss and embrace the values and living them is the intention of this family journey.

The Holy Bible and Translations

Leading Scripture comes from the New American Standard Bible, (NASB), The Passion Translation, (TPT) and the International Children's Bible, (ICB). These translations are used to ensure that all family members can access God's word to understand the truths of HIS word.

The New American Standard Bible is a literal translation from the original texts, well suited to study because of its accurate translation of the original scrolls. It follows the style of the King James Version but uses modern English for words that have fallen out of use or changed their meanings.

These translations were chosen to:

- *Be true to the original Hebrew, Aramaic, and Greek*
- *Be grammatically correct*
- *Be understandable*
- *Give the Lord Jesus Christ His proper place*

Opening Prayer for Guidance:

Heavenly Father, as we begin this journey, we ask for Your wisdom and guidance. Holy Spirit, lead us into all truth, and help us to grasp the depth of Your love and the richness of our inheritance in the Kingdom of God. Strengthen our faith, and embolden us to live out Your Word in every aspect of our lives. In Jesus' name we pray, Amen.

Family Declaration:

Together, we declare: We are citizens of God's Kingdom, members of His royal family. Rooted in Christ, we commit to representing His love, grace, and righteousness in all we do. Our lives are a testament to the Kingdom's values, and through our actions, love and family, we aim to glorify our Heavenly Father as his Royal Kingdom Family.

Let this devotional bible study journey be a time of deepening connection, fellowship and relationship, with God and with each other as a family. As we seek first His Kingdom, may our hearts and homes be filled with His peace, joy, and abundance.

Day 1: Embracing Our Royal Identity

Welcome to Day 1 of our 30-day family devotional journey! Today's scripture from Ephesians 2:19 reminds us of our royal identity as citizens of God's household. Let's dive into how we can practically apply this truth to our lives.

Scripture: Ephesians 2:19

"So then you are no longer strangers and foreigners, but you are fellow citizens with the [a]saints, and are of God's household," (*NASB*)

'So, you are not foreigners or guests, but rather you are the children of the city of the holy ones, with all the rights as family members of the household of God. (TPT)

So now you, non-Jews are not visitors or strangers. Now you are citizens together with God's holy people. You belong to God's family. (ICB)

Envisioning a Practical Connection:

Imagine waking up every morning knowing that you belong to the King of Kings. As adults, this means understanding our responsibility to represent His love, grace, and truth in every interaction. For children, tweens, and teens, it's about recognizing that you are part of a special family with a unique purpose—to shine God's light wherever you go.

Clarifying the Teaching:

This scripture teaches us that we are not alone; we are part of God's royal family. It urges us to update our mindset, embracing our identity as beloved children of the King. As a family, let's remind each other daily of who we are in Christ and the significance of our role in His Kingdom. We can remind each other by how we talk to each other, encourage each other and how we address each other by the names we use.

Benefits of Living as God's Royal Family:

Living according to God's wisdom and principles grants us the privilege of experiencing His abundant life. As citizens of His Kingdom, we have authority, rights, and privileges that come with being heirs of Christ. Let's embrace this truth and walk confidently in our royal identity.

Family Reflection:

Adult Perspective: Consider and think carefully about how your understanding of being a citizen of God's household impacts your daily decisions and interactions with others.

Child Perspective: Imagine what it means to be part of God's royal family. How can you show love and kindness to those around you?

Tween Perspective: Reflect and think carefully about how knowing your royal identity affects your friendships and relationships with peers. How can you be a positive influence in your circle?

Teen Perspective: Ponder, consider and think about, the responsibility that comes with being a citizen of God's Kingdom. How can you use your influence to make a difference in your school or community?

Transforming Our Mind:

Think about practical ways to align your thoughts and actions with your royal identity. How can you show love, grace, and truth to those around you, reflecting the character of your Heavenly Father?

Additional Reading:

Explore these scriptures related to the theme. Read out loud, then share your thoughts about what the scriptures are saying and teaching us, especially about God and who we are as children of God:

1 Peter 2:9 (NASB) - "But you are a chosen race, a royal priesthood, a holy nation, a people for God's own possession, so that you may proclaim the excellencies of Him who has called you out of darkness into His marvelous light."

Matthew 5:14 (Passion Translation) - "Your lives light up the world. Let others see your light from a distance, for how can you hide a city that stands on a hilltop?"

Romans 8:16-17 (NASB) - "The Spirit Himself testifies with our spirit that we are children of God, and if children, heirs also, heirs of God and fellow heirs with Christ."

Family commitment: Today I will intentionally...

Family Declaration:

As a family, let's declare together: "We are citizens of God's Kingdom, heirs of Christ, and part of His royal family. We embrace our identity and purpose, shining God's light wherever we go."

Thanksgiving and Prayer for Guidance:

Thank You, Heavenly Father, for adopting us into Your family. Heavenly Father, we come before you, asking for Your Holy Spirit to lead and guide us. Grant us grace, insight, and understanding as we navigate our lives as members of Your royal family. Help us to walk in Your truth and love." In Jesus' name, we pray. Amen.

Day 2: Seeking First the Kingdom

Welcome to Day 2 of our family devotional journey! Today, we focus on the importance of prioritizing God's Kingdom above all else. Let's explore how we can practically apply this principle to our lives

Scripture: Matthew 6:33

"But seek first His kingdom and His righteousness, and all these things will be added to you." (NASB)

"'So above all, constantly seek God's kingdom and his righteousness, then all these less important things will be given to you abundantly.' (TPT)

"The thing you should want most is God's kingdom and doing what God wants. Then all these other things you need will be given to you." (ICB)

Envisioning a Practical Connection:

Imagine starting each day with the intention of seeking God's Kingdom first. As adults, this means aligning our goals and ambitions with God's will, trusting that He will provide for all our needs. For children, tweens, and teens, it's about understanding that putting God first in everything brings blessings and fulfillment beyond measure.

Clarifying the Teaching:

This scripture teaches us that when we prioritize God's Kingdom and His righteousness, everything else falls into place. It urges us to update our mindset, shifting our focus from worldly pursuits to eternal values. As a family, let's encourage each other to seek God's Kingdom above all else, trusting in His provision and guidance.

Benefits of Seeking First the Kingdom:

Living with a Kingdom mindset brings peace, joy, and abundance. When we prioritize God's Kingdom, we experience His presence and provision in every aspect of our lives. Let's embrace the blessings that come from seeking God first and foremost. As we draw closer to God he draws closer to us and reveals himself as Father and friend.

Family Reflection:

Adult Perspective: Reflect on how you can seek God's Kingdom in your daily activities, decisions, and relationships. Consider areas where you may need to realign your priorities to honor God.

Child Perspective: Think about what it means to seek God's Kingdom first as a child. How can you prioritize spending time with God and obeying His Word in your everyday life?

Tween Perspective: Consider the distractions that compete for your attention and how you can refocus on seeking God's Kingdom above all else. What changes can you make to put God first in your schedule and priorities?

Teen Perspective: Reflect on the pressures and demands of teenage life. How can you resist the temptation to prioritize worldly pursuits and instead seek God's Kingdom with all your heart, mind, and strength?

Transforming Our Mind: Think about practical ways to prioritize God's Kingdom in your daily routine. How can you incorporate prayer, scripture reading, Bible study, and serving others into your schedule to ensure that God remains the focal point of your life?

Additional Reading:

Explore these scriptures related to the theme. Read out loud, then share your thoughts about what the scriptures are saying and teaching us, especially about God, his values, his virtues and who we are as children of God:

Luke 12:31-32 (NASB) - "But seek His kingdom, and these things will be provided to you. Do not be afraid, little flock, because your Father has chosen to give you the kingdom."

Colossians 3:1-2 (Passion Translation) - "Christ's resurrection is your resurrection too. This is why we are to yearn for all that is above, for that's where Christ sits enthroned at the place of all power, honor, and authority! Yes, feast on all the treasures of the heavenly realm and fill your thoughts with heavenly realities, and not with the distractions of the natural realm."

Psalm 37:4 (NASB) - "Delight yourself in the Lord, and He will give you the desires of your heart."
Psalms 37:4 (ICB) "Enjoy serving the Lord. And he will give you what you want."

Family commitment: Today I will intentionally...

Family Declaration:

Together, let's declare: "We seek first the Kingdom of God and His righteousness. We trust that as we prioritize God's Kingdom, He will provide for all our needs and lead us into an abundant life."

Thanksgiving and Prayer for Guidance:

Thank You, Heavenly Father, for the promise that when we seek Your Kingdom first, all things will be added unto us. Heavenly Father, we come before you, asking for Your Holy Spirit to help us seek Your Kingdom above all else. Give us the desire, wisdom and strength to prioritize Your will and righteousness in everything we do. Help us to trust in Your provision and guidance." In Jesus' name, we pray. Amen.

Day 3: Trusting in God's Provision

Welcome to Day 3 of our family devotional journey! Today, we focus on trusting in God's provision for all our needs. Let's explore how we can practically apply this truth to our lives.

Scripture: Philippians 4:19

"And my God will supply all your needs according to His riches in glory in Christ Jesus."(NASB)

'I am convinced that my God will fully satisfy every need you have, for I have seen the abundant riches of glory revealed to me through Jesus Christ! ' (TPT)

"My God will use his wonderful riches in Christ Jesus to give you everything you need." (ICB)

Envisioning a Practical Connection:

Imagine living each day with the assurance that God will supply all your needs. As adults, this means releasing worry and anxiety about financial concerns, health issues, or family matters, knowing that God is faithful to provide. For children, tweens, and teens, it's about learning to trust God with every aspect of your life, believing that He cares for you and will take care of you.

Clarifying the Teaching:

This scripture reassures us that God is our ultimate provider. It urges us to update our mindset, shifting from a mindset of scarcity and fear to one of abundance and trust in God's faithfulness. As a family, let's remind each other daily of God's promise to supply all our needs according to His riches in glory.

Benefits of Trusting in God's Provision:

Trusting in God's provision brings peace and contentment, knowing that He is in control and will take care of us. It frees us from the burden of worrying about the future and allows us to live with confidence and joy in the present moment. Let's embrace the blessings that come from trusting in God's provision and faithfulness.

Family Reflection:

Adult Perspective: Reflect on areas of your life where you struggle to trust God's provision. Surrender those areas to Him in prayer and ask for the faith to believe that He will provide for all your needs.

Child Perspective: Think about times when you have seen God provide for you and your family. How does knowing that God is your provider give you peace and confidence?

Tween Perspective: Consider the things you worry about and how trusting in God's provision can alleviate your anxiety. How can you remind yourself daily of God's faithfulness?

Teen Perspective: Reflect on the pressures and uncertainties you face as a teenager. How can trusting in God's provision give you hope and confidence for the future?

Transforming Our Mind:

Think about practical ways to trust in God's provision in your daily life. How can you cultivate a mindset of abundance and faithfulness, even in the midst of challenges and uncertainties? Declaring God's truths and verbally affirming, through affirmations, what God has said about who he is, what he does and what he will do for his children can be a great starting point to grow in our confidence and faith.

Additional Reading:

Explore these scriptures related to the theme. Read out loud, then share your thoughts about what the scriptures are saying and teaching us, especially about God, King Jesus and who we are as children of God:

Matthew 6:26 (NASB) - "Look at the birds of the air, that they do not sow, nor reap nor gather into barns, and yet your heavenly Father feeds them. Are you not worth much more than they?"

Psalm 23:1 (Passion Translation) - "'Yahweh is my best friend and my shepherd. I always have more than enough.

Luke 12:22-24 (ICB) - Jesus said to his followers, "So I tell you, don't worry about the food you need to live. Don't worry about the clothes you need for your body. Life is more important than food. And the body is more important than clothes. Look at the birds. They don't plant or harvest. They don't save food in houses or barns. But God takes care of them. And you are worth much more than birds.

Family commitment: Today I will intentionally...

Family Declaration:

Together, let's declare: "We trust in God's provision for all our needs. We believe that He is faithful to take care of us and will supply everything we need according to His riches in glory."

Thanksgiving and Prayer for Guidance:

Heavenly Father, we come before you, thanking you for your promise to supply all our needs according to your riches in glory. Thank You, Heavenly Father, for your provision and faithfulness. Help us to trust in You for all of our needs, to know and believe that You will supply abundantly and according to Your riches in glory. Help us to trust in your provision and have faith that you will take care of us in every situation. In Jesus' name, we pray. Amen.

Day 4: Living in Contentment

Welcome to Day 4 of our family devotional journey! Today, we focus on the importance of living in contentment, trusting in God's provision and faithfulness. Let's explore how we can practically apply this truth to our lives.

Scripture: Philippians 4:11-13

'Not that I speak from need, for I have learned to be content in whatever circumstances I am. I know how to get along with little, and I also know how to live in prosperity; in any and every circumstance I have learned the secret of being filled and going hungry, both of having abundance and suffering need. I can do all things through Him who strengthens me. '(NASB)

"I know what it means to lack, and I know what it means to experience overwhelming abundance. For I'm trained in the secret of overcoming all things, whether in fullness or in hunger. And I find that the strength of Christ's explosive power infuses me to conquer every difficulty. (TPT)

I am telling you this, but it is not because I need anything. I have learned to be satisfied with the things I have and with everything that happens. I know how to live when I am poor. And I know how to live when I have plenty. I have learned the secret of being happy at any time in everything that happens. I have learned to be happy when I have enough to eat and when I do not have enough to eat. I have learned to be happy when I have all that I need and when I do not have the things I need. I can do all things through Christ because he gives me strength. (ICB)

Envisioning a Practical Connection:

Imagine feeling content and satisfied with what you have, knowing that God will never leave you or forsake you. As adults, this means releasing the grip of materialism and finding joy and fulfillment in God's presence and provision. For children, tweens, and teens, it's about learning to appreciate what you have and trusting that God will take care of your needs.

Clarifying the Teaching:

This scripture reminds us that true contentment comes from trusting in God's faithfulness, not from worldly possessions or wealth. It urges us to shift from a mindset of always wanting more to one of gratitude and satisfaction in God's provision. As a family, let's cultivate an attitude of contentment, recognizing that true riches come from knowing and trusting in God.

Benefits of Living in Contentment:

Living in contentment brings peace and freedom from the pursuit of material possessions. It allows us to enjoy the blessings that God has given us and to find satisfaction in His presence. Let's embrace the joy and fulfillment that come from trusting in God's provision and faithfulness. His provisions are not just material things but things money can't buy. This also helps us to focus our thoughts on appreciation of all that he has provided, not taking what we do have in our lives for granted.

Family Reflection:

Adult Perspective: Reflect on areas of your life where you struggle with contentment. Surrender those areas to God and ask Him to help you find joy and satisfaction in His presence and provision.

Child Perspective: Think about times when you have felt content and happy with what you have. How does knowing that God will never leave you or forsake you give you peace and comfort?

Tween Perspective: Consider the things you often desire or wish you had. How can you cultivate a spirit of contentment and gratitude for what you already have?

Teen Perspective: Reflect on the pressures and influences that may tempt you to pursue material possessions or wealth. How can you resist those temptations and comparisons of others and find true contentment in God as our loving father and source alone?

Transforming Our Mind:

Think about practical ways to cultivate contentment in your daily life. How can you focus on gratitude and trust in God's provision, rather than always wanting more?

Additional Reading:

Explore these scriptures related to the theme. Read out loud, then share your thoughts about what the scriptures are saying and teaching us, especially about God, his values, his virtues and who we are as children of God:

> *Hebrews 13:5 (NASB) Make sure that* your character is free from the love of money, being content with what you have; for He Himself has said, "I WILL NEVER DESERT YOU, NOR WILL I EVER ABANDON YOU,"

> *1 Timothy 6:6 (NASB)* - 'But godliness actually is a means of great gain when accompanied by contentment. '

> *Hebrews 13:5 (ICB)*"Keep your lives free from the love of money. And be satisfied with what you have. God has said, "I will never leave you; I will never abandon you."

> *Psalm 16:5-6 (ICB)* -'No, the Lord is all I need. He takes care of me. My share in life has been pleasant. My part has been beautiful.'

Family commitment: Today I will intentionally...

Family Declaration:

Together, let's declare: "We choose to live in contentment, trusting in God's provision and faithfulness. We find joy and satisfaction in His presence, knowing that He will never desert us or abandon us."

Thanksgiving and Prayer for Guidance:

Thank You, Heavenly Father, for your provision and faithfulness. Heavenly Father, we come before you, asking for your help to cultivate and develop contentment in our hearts and minds. Help us to find joy and satisfaction in your presence and all your provisions, knowing that you will never leave us or forsake us. Help us to trust and be content with what we have, that we have true joy and satisfaction in You, knowing that You will never leave us or abandon us. Thank you for your faithfulness, we believe you. In Jesus' name, we pray. Amen.

Day 5: Walking in Humility

Welcome to Day 5 of our family devotional journey! Today, we focus on the importance of walking in humility before our God. Let's explore how we can practically apply this truth to our lives.

Scripture:1 Peter 5:5-6

"Clothe yourselves with humility toward one another, for God is opposed to the proud, but gives grace to the humble. Therefore humble yourselves under the mighty hand of God, that He may exalt you at the proper time." (NASB)

'In the same way, the younger ones should willingly support the leadership of the elders. In every relationship, each of you must wrap around yourself the apron of a humble servant. Because God resists you when you are proud but multiplies grace and favor when you are humble. If you bow low in God's awesome presence, he will eventually exalt you as you leave the timing in his hands.'(TPT)

'In the same way, younger men should be willing to be under older men. And all of you should be very humble with each other. God is against the proud, but he gives grace to the humble. So be humble under God's powerful hand. Then he will lift you up when the right time comes. '(ICB)

Envisioning a Practical Connection:

Imagine walking through life with humility, recognizing our dependence on God and our responsibility to live justly and kindly towards others. As adults, this means recognizing our limitations and strengths, and willingly submitting to God's guidance and authority. For children, tweens, and teens, it's about understanding that true greatness comes from serving others with a humble heart, following the example of Jesus.

Clarifying the Teaching:

This scripture reminds us that God desires our obedience, justice, and kindness, but above all, He desires for us to walk humbly with Him. It urges us to shift from pride and self-sufficiency to humility and dependence on God's wisdom and grace. God wants to provide for his children with good things. He wants us to depend on him, acknowledge him as our God and loving Father. He wants us to seek him, trust him and receive from him all that we need. As a family, let's strive to walk in humility, acknowledging God's sovereignty and seeking His guidance in all we do.

Benefits of Walking in Humility:

Walking in humility allows us to experience deeper intimacy with God and healthier relationships with others. It opens the door to God's wisdom and grace, leading to a life of peace, joy, and purpose. Let's embrace the blessings that come from walking humbly with our God. This concept of humility is valued very differently in the Family of God from the culture of the world. This world promotes and encourages pride, being better than others by putting others down, and being self-centered and seeing everyone as lower or less than you. Someone being better at something does not make you less. As God's royal family, each of us are #1 in God's eyes, a family of many beloved Kings and Queens, Princes and Princesses. Independence and self-sufficiency are other concepts that are opposite of the Kingdom of God values and ways of living and being. In God's family, with his power and grace, we have all sufficiency in all things at all times

Family Reflection:

Adult Perspective: Reflect on areas of your life where pride and self-sufficiency may be hindering your walk with God. Surrender those areas to Him and ask for His grace to cultivate humility in your heart.

Child Perspective: Think about times when you have felt proud or boastful. How can you cultivate a spirit of humility and service, by following the examples of Jesus? Jesus' example helped people to see and understand humility, the way of the Kingdom and learn how to serve one another.

Tween Perspective: Consider the ways you interact with others and how humility can strengthen your relationships. How can you show kindness and compassion to those around you, reflecting God's love?

Teen Perspective: Reflect on the pressures and expectations you face as a teenager. How can walking in humility help you navigate these challenges and honor God with your actions?

Transforming Our Mind:

Think about practical ways to cultivate humility in your daily life. How can you practice humility in your relationships, your attitude towards others, your view of others and your response to difficult situations?

Additional Reading:

Explore these scriptures related to the theme. Read out loud, then share your thoughts about what the scriptures are saying and teaching us, especially about God, his values, this Kingdom virtue and who we are as children of God:

Proverbs 11:2 (NASB) - "When pride comes, then comes dishonor, but with the humble is wisdom."

James 4:6 (Passion Translation) - "But he continues to pour out more and more grace upon us. For it says, God resists you when you are proud but continually pours out grace when you are humble."

Micah 6:8 (ICB) "The Lord has told you what is good. He has told you what he wants from you: Do what is right to other people. Love being kind to others. And live humbly, trusting your God.

Family Declaration:

Together, let's declare: "We choose to walk humbly with our God, acknowledging His sovereignty and seeking His guidance in all we do. We strive to live justly, love kindness, and walk humbly before God, our Heavenly Father."

Thanksgiving and Prayer for Guidance:

Thank You, Heavenly Father, for Your grace and guidance. Heavenly Father, we come before you, asking for your help to walk humbly with You. Help us to walk humbly with You God, seeking Your wisdom and grace in all we do. In You God, we find strength, peace, and purpose. Give us the grace to recognize our dependence on You and to depend on you. Give us the strength to follow Your guidance in all we do. In Jesus' name, we pray. Amen.

Day 6: Embracing Forgiveness

Welcome to Day 6 of our family devotional journey! Today, we focus on the importance of embracing forgiveness as a vital aspect of our walk with God. Let's explore how we can practically apply this truth to our lives.

Scripture: Colossians 3:13

> "Bearing with one another, and forgiving each other, whoever has a complaint against anyone; just as the Lord forgave you, so also should you." (NASB)

> 'Tolerate the weaknesses of those in the family of faith, forgiving one another in the same way you have been graciously forgiven by Jesus Christ. If you find fault with someone, release this same gift of forgiveness to them. ' (TPT)

> Do not be angry with each other, but forgive each other. If someone does wrong to you, then forgive him. Forgive each other because the Lord forgave you. (ICB)

Envisioning a Practical Connection:

Imagine living in a family where forgiveness flows freely, where conflicts are resolved, and relationships are strengthened. As adults, this means extending grace and mercy to those who have wronged us, just as the Lord forgave us. For children, tweens, and teens, it's about learning to let go of hurt and resentment and choosing to forgive others, following the example of Jesus.

Clarifying the Teaching:

This scripture reminds us of the forgiveness we have received from the Lord and urges us to extend that same forgiveness to others. It urges us to shift from holding onto grudges and bitterness to offering grace and reconciliation. As a family, let's embrace forgiveness as a foundational principle of our relationships, reflecting the love and mercy of our Heavenly Father.

Benefits of Embracing Forgiveness:

Embracing forgiveness brings freedom and healing to our hearts and relationships. It releases us from the burden of carrying resentment and allows us to experience the joy and peace that come from reconciliation. Unforgiveness negatively impacts our physical and emotional health and future relationships with others. Unforgiveness is linked to higher incidences of stress, heart disease, high blood pressure, lowered immune response, anxiety, depression, and other health issues.

Unforgiveness keeps that pain alive. Unforgiveness never lets that wound heal, and you go through life reminding yourself of what was done to you, revisiting the pain, which grows into a life of accumulating bad feelings and negative thoughts. Let's embrace the blessings that come from extending forgiveness to others, knowing that it reflects the heart of God and it is beneficial to our future relationships, heart, feelings and health.

Family Reflection:

Adult Perspective: Reflect on times when you struggled to forgive others. Surrender those hurts to God and ask for His help to extend forgiveness, just as He has forgiven you.

Child Perspective: Think about a time when you felt hurt by someone's words or actions. How did it feel to forgive them, and how did it change your relationship with them?

Tween Perspective: Consider the importance of forgiveness in your friendships and family relationships. How can you actively choose to forgive others and seek reconciliation when conflicts arise?

Teen Perspective: Reflect on the impact of holding onto grudges and bitterness in your life. How can choosing to forgive others bring freedom and healing to your heart and relationships?

Transforming Our Mind:

Think about practical ways to cultivate a spirit of forgiveness in your family. How can you create a culture of grace and reconciliation, where forgiveness is freely given and received?

Additional Reading:

Explore these scriptures related to the theme. Read out loud, then share your thoughts about what the scriptures are saying and teaching us, especially about God, Jesus Christ, this Kingdom virtue and who we are as children of God:

Matthew 6:14-15 (NASB) - " For if you forgive other people for their offenses (wrongdoings), your heavenly Father will also forgive you. But if you do not forgive other people, then your Father will not forgive your offenses (wrongdoings)."

Ephesians 4:32 (TPT) - "But instead be kind and affectionate toward one another. Has God graciously forgiven you? Then graciously forgive one another in the depths of Christ's love."

Luke 6:37 (TPT) - "'Jesus said, Forsake the habit of criticizing and judging others, and you will not be criticized and judged in return. Don't condemn others and you will not be condemned. Forgive over and over, and you will be forgiven over and over. '

Luke 6:37 (ICB) - "Don't judge other people, and you will not be judged. Don't accuse others of being guilty, and you will not be accused of being guilty. Forgive other people, and you will be forgiven."

Family commitment: Today I will intentionally...

Family Declaration:

Together, let's declare: "We choose to embrace forgiveness, extending grace and mercy to others just as the Lord has forgiven us. We release the burden of resentment, grudges and walk in freedom, forgiveness and reconciliation."

Thanksgiving and Prayer for Guidance:

Thank You, Heavenly Father, for the forgiveness we have received through Jesus Christ. Heavenly Father, we come before you, asking for your help to embrace forgiveness in our hearts and relationships. Help us to choose to forgive others as You Lord have forgiven each of us. Give us the grace to extend forgiveness to others, just as you have forgiven us. Help us to walk in this freedom and reconciliation of restored friendly relations with you and others. In You God, we find healing and peace from forgiveness. In Jesus' name, we pray and we praise You for your faithfulness, Amen.

Day 7: Cultivating Gratitude

Welcome to Day 7 of our family devotional journey! Today, we focus on cultivating an attitude of gratitude, recognizing God's goodness and faithfulness in every circumstance. Let's explore how we can practically apply this truth to our lives.

Scripture: 1 Thessalonians 5:18

> "In everything give thanks; for this is God's will for you in Christ Jesus." (NASB)

> 'And in the midst of everything be always giving thanks, for this is God's perfect plan for you in Christ Jesus. '(TPT)

> "Give thanks whatever happens. That is what God wants for you in Christ Jesus." (ICB)

Envisioning a Practical Connection:

Imagine living each day with a heart overflowing with gratitude, finding joy and beauty in the smallest blessings. As adults, this means intentionally pausing to give thanks for God's provision, protection, and presence in our lives. For children, tweens, and teens, it's about learning to see God's handiwork in the world around you and expressing gratitude for His love and care.

Clarifying the Teaching:

This scripture reminds us that gratitude is not dependent on our circumstances but is a choice we can make in every situation. It urges us to shift from complaining and discontent to a posture of thankfulness and praise. As a family, let's cultivate a spirit of gratitude, recognizing God's goodness and faithfulness in all things.

Benefits of Cultivating Gratitude:

Cultivating gratitude brings joy, peace, happiness and contentment to our hearts. It shifts our focus from what we lack to what we have, fostering a spirit of abundance and generosity. Mindfulness and gratitude can help improve overall well-being by changing perceptions, attitudes, thoughts, feelings which helps you to see things through a lens of positivity and also makes you feel happier and more fulfilled.

Let's embrace the blessings that come from giving thanks in all circumstances, knowing that it aligns us with God's will for our lives and is good for our well-being and happiness.

Family Reflection:

Adult Perspective: Reflect on the blessings in your life for which you are grateful. Take time to thank God for His goodness and faithfulness, even in the midst of challenges.

Child Perspective: Think about something that brings you joy or makes you smile. How can you express gratitude to God for this blessing in your life?

Tween Perspective: Consider the people in your life who have made a difference or shown you kindness. How can you show appreciation and gratitude for them?

Teen Perspective: Reflect on the role of gratitude in your mental and emotional well-being. How can cultivating gratitude help you navigate the ups and downs of teenage life?

Transforming Our Mind:

Think about practical ways to cultivate and increase gratitude in your daily life. How can you incorporate moments of thanksgiving and praise into your routine, even during busy or challenging times? Gratitude affects our attitude!

Additional Reading:

Explore these scriptures related to the theme. Read out loud, then share your thoughts about what the scriptures are saying and teaching us, especially about God, Jesus Christ, this Kingdom virtue and who we are as children of God:

Psalm 100:4 (NASB) - "Enter His gates with thanksgiving and His courts with praise. Give thanks to Him, bless His name."

Philippians 4:6-7 (Passion Translation) - "'Don't be pulled in different directions or worried about a thing. Be saturated in prayer throughout each day, offering your faith-filled requests before God with overflowing gratitude. Tell him every detail of your life, then God's wonderful peace that transcends human understanding, will guard your heart and mind through Jesus Christ. '

Psalm 106:1 (NASB) - "Praise the Lord! Oh give thanks to the Lord, for He is good; for His mercy (graciousness, lovingkindness , compassion) is everlasting."

Psalm 106:1 (ICB) - "Praise the Lord! Thank the Lord because he is good. His love continues forever.

Family commitment: Today I will intentionally...

Family Declaration:

Together, let's declare: "We choose to cultivate gratitude, giving thanks in all circumstances, for this is God's will for us in Christ Jesus. We acknowledge Your goodness and faithfulness in every aspect of our lives, Heavenly Father. We are grateful for every blessing in our life, big, medium and small".

Thanksgiving and Prayer for Guidance:

Thank You, Heavenly Father, for your abundant blessings and provision. Heavenly Father, we come before you, thanking you for your countless blessings in our lives. Help us to notice, acknowledge and be grateful for every blessing in our lives, big and small. Help us to cultivate and develop an attitude of gratitude, recognizing your goodness and faithfulness in all things and giving thanks in all circumstances. Holy Spirit, help us to notice the blessings and to express gratitude. Help us to develop a heart of gratitude which positively affects our attitude, In Jesus' name, we pray. Amen.

Day 8: Seeking Wisdom

Welcome to Day 8 of our family devotional journey! Today, we focus on the importance of seeking wisdom from God, who generously gives to all who ask. Let's explore how we can practically apply this truth to our lives.

Scripture: James 1:5

> "But if any of you lacks wisdom, let him ask of God, who gives to all generously and without reproach, and it will be given to him." (NASB)

> 'And if anyone longs to be wise, ask God for wisdom and he will give it! He won't see your lack of wisdom as an opportunity to scold you over your failures but he will overwhelm your failures with his generous grace. ' (TPT)

> "But if any of you needs wisdom, you should ask God for it. God is generous. He enjoys giving to all people, so God will give you wisdom." (ICB)

Envisioning a Practical Connection:

Imagine facing life's challenges with confidence and discernment (obtaining spiritual guidance and understanding) knowing that you have access to divine wisdom from God. As adults, this means humbly acknowledging our need for wisdom and seeking God's guidance in decision-making and problem-solving. For children, tweens, and teens, it's about learning to trust God's wisdom above our own understanding and seeking His direction in all areas of life.

Clarifying the Teaching:

This scripture reminds us that wisdom is a gift from God, available to all who ask in faith. It urges us to shift from relying solely on our own understanding to seeking God's wisdom and guidance in every situation. Wisdom is seeing the world from **God's** perspective and then applying that perspective to our lives. As a family, let's encourage each other to seek wisdom from God, knowing that He generously provides it to those who ask and believe to receive.

Benefits of Seeking Wisdom:

Seeking wisdom from God leads to sound decision-making, fruitful relationships, and a deeper understanding of God's will for our lives. It empowers us to navigate life's complexities with clarity and discernment, ultimately leading to a life of purpose and fulfillment. Let's embrace the blessings that come from seeking wisdom from God, knowing that it is the key to living a life that honors Him and helps us make wise decisions that minimize negative outcomes in our lives.

Family Reflection:

Adult Perspective: Reflect on a recent decision you had to make and whether you sought God's wisdom in the process. How can you prioritize seeking God's guidance in all areas of your life?

Child Perspective: Think about a time when you needed help understanding something or making a choice. How can you ask God for wisdom and trust Him to guide you in the right direction?

Tween Perspective: Consider the challenges you face as you grow older and encounter new experiences. How can seeking wisdom from God help you make wise choices and navigate life's ups and downs?

Teen Perspective: Reflect on the pressures and decisions you're facing as a teenager. How can seeking wisdom from God equip you to make choices that honor Him and lead to a fulfilling life?

Transforming Our Mind:

Think about practical ways to seek wisdom from God in your daily life. How can you prioritize prayer, reading the Bible, and seeking counsel from mature believers to gain godly wisdom and understanding?   Seeking wisdom, insight and discernment in situations and decisions is a practice of maturity and helps us to become wise.

Additional Reading:

Explore these scriptures related to the theme. Read out loud, then share your thoughts about what the scriptures are saying and teaching us, especially about God and who we are as children of God:

Proverbs 2:6 (NASB) - "For the Lord gives wisdom; from His mouth come knowledge and understanding."

Proverbs 3:5-6 (Passion Translation) - "Trust in the Lord completely, and do not rely on your own opinions. With all your heart, rely on him to guide you, and he will lead you in every decision you make. Become intimate with him in whatever you do, and he will lead you wherever you go."

Proverbs 4:7 (NASB) - "'The beginning of wisdom is: Acquire wisdom; And with all your possessions, acquire understanding. "

Proverbs 4:7 (ICB) - Wisdom is the most important thing. So get wisdom. If it costs everything you have, get understanding.

Family commitment: Today I will intentionally...

Family Declaration:

Together, let's declare: "We seek wisdom from God, knowing that He generously gives to all who ask. We trust in His guidance and rely on His wisdom to navigate life's challenges and decisions."

Thanksgiving and Prayer for Guidance:

Thank You, Heavenly Father, for the gift of wisdom that You freely give to all who ask and believe. Heavenly Father, we come before you, asking for wisdom and understanding in all areas of our lives. Help us to seek wisdom from You in all areas of our lives, trusting in Your guidance and understanding. Help us to have humility to seek Your guidance in everything we do. Grant us with discernment, to determine things well and to make wise choices. In Jesus' name, we pray. Amen.

Day 9: Walking in Love

Welcome to Day 9 of our family devotional journey! Today, we focus on the transformative power of walking in love, following the example of Christ's sacrificial love for us. Let's explore how we can practically apply this truth to our lives.

Scripture: 1 Corinthians 13:4-7

> "Love is patient, love is kind and is not jealous; love does not brag and is not arrogant, does not act unbecomingly; it does not seek its own, is not provoked, does not take into account a wrong suffered, does not rejoice in unrighteousness, but rejoices with the truth; bears all things, believes all things, hopes all things, endures all things."*(NASB)*

> 'Love is large and incredibly patient. Love is gentle and consistently kind to all. It refuses to be jealous when blessing comes to someone else . Love does not brag about one's achievements nor inflate its own importance. Love does not traffic in shame and disrespect, nor selfishly seek its own honor. Love is not easily irritated or quick to take offense. Love joyfully celebrates honesty and finds no delight in what is wrong. Love is a safe place of shelter, for it never stops believing the best for others. Love never takes failure as defeat, for it never gives up.' (TPT)

> Love is patient and kind. Love is not jealous, it does not brag, and it is not proud. Love is not rude, is not selfish, and does not become angry easily. Love does not remember wrongs done against it. Love takes no pleasure in evil, but rejoices over the truth. Love patiently accepts all things. It always trusts, always hopes, and always continues strong. (ICB)

Envisioning a Practical Connection:

Imagine a world where love guides every action and decision, where compassion and kindness reign supreme. As adults, this means embodying the selfless love of Christ in our relationships, interactions, and attitudes towards others. For children, tweens, and teens, it's about learning to see others through the lens of love and treating them with kindness, empathy, and respect.

Clarifying the Teaching:

These scriptures remind us that love is not just a feeling but a way of life, demonstrated by Christ's ministry and ultimate sacrifice on the cross. It urges us to shift from self-centeredness and indifference to a lifestyle of sacrificial love and service. As a family, let's strive to walk in love, imitating the example of Christ and reflecting His love to the world around us.

Benefits of Walking in Love:

Walking in love transforms our hearts, relationships, and communities. It breaks down barriers, fosters unity, and brings healing and restoration to brokenness. Let's embrace the blessings that come from walking in love, knowing that it is the greatest commandment and the essence of our calling as followers of Christ. Love is showing kindness, being cordial and being patient; patient with God as he works with others in their journey of life and patient with others as they grow and mature.

Family Reflection:

Adult Perspective: Reflect on opportunities to demonstrate love in your daily life, whether through acts of kindness, words of encouragement, or sacrificial giving. How can you embody the love of Christ in your relationships and interactions with others?

Child Perspective: Think about someone in your life who could use a little extra love and kindness. How can you show them love in a tangible, real way, following the example of Jesus?

Tween Perspective: Consider the importance of treating others with kindness and respect, even when it's challenging. How can you show love to those who may be difficult to love, reflecting the unconditional love of Christ?

Teen Perspective: Reflect on the impact of love in your friendships, family dynamics, and interactions with others. How can you prioritize walking in love in all areas of your life, following the example of Christ's sacrificial love?

Transforming Our Mind:

Think about practical ways to walk in love in your daily life. How can you cultivate a heart of compassion, kindness, and empathy towards others, seeking to imitate the love of Christ in all you do?

Additional Reading:

Explore these scriptures related to the theme. Read out loud, then share your thoughts about what the scriptures are saying and teaching us, especially about God, Jesus Christ, the Kingdom virtue and value of Love and who we are as children of God:

1 John 4:7-8 (NASB) - "Beloved, let us love one another, for love is from God; and everyone who loves is born of God and knows God. The one who does not love does not know God, for God is love."

John 13:34-35 (Passion Translation) - "So I give you now a new commandment: Love each other just as much as I have loved you. For when you demonstrate the same love I have for you by loving one another, everyone will know that you're my true followers."

Ephesians 5:1-2 '(TPT)'Be imitators of God in everything you do, for then you will represent your Father as his beloved sons and daughters. And continue to walk surrendered to the extravagant love of Christ, for he surrendered his life as a sacrifice for us. His great love for us was pleasing to God, like an aroma of adoration—a sweet healing fragrance.

Family commitment: Today I will intentionally...

Family Declaration:

Together, let's declare: "We choose to walk in love, just as Christ loved us and gave Himself up for us. May Jesus' love compel us to love others sacrificially and selflessly."

Thanksgiving and Prayer for Guidance:

Thank You, Heavenly Father, for the gift of love demonstrated through Jesus Christ. Heavenly Father, we come before you, asking for your help to walk in love as Christ loved us. Help us to walk in love, imitating the selfless and sacrificial love of Christ in all we do. Fill our hearts with your love and the love of Christ, that we may overflow with compassion, kindness, and grace towards others. Let your love guide our actions, attitudes, and relationships." In Jesus' name, we pray. Amen.

Day 10: Growing in Unity

Welcome to Day 10 of our family devotional journey! Today, we focus on the beauty and significance of unity among believers. Let's explore how we can practically apply this truth to our lives.

Scripture: Psalm 133:1

> "Behold, how good and how pleasant it is for brothers to live together in unity!"(NASB)

> 'How truly wonderful and delightful it is to see brothers and sisters living together in sweet unity! ' (TPT)

> "It is good and pleasant when God's people live together in peace!"(ICB)

Envisioning a Practical Connection:

Imagine a family where unity reigns supreme, where differences are celebrated, and love binds hearts together. As adults, this means fostering an atmosphere of unity within our families, communities, and churches, embracing diversity and building bridges of understanding and compassion. For children, tweens, and teens, it's about valuing each other's unique differences, gifts and perspectives, seeking harmony and peace in all relationships.

Clarifying the Teaching:

This scripture reminds us of the goodness and pleasantness of dwelling together in unity. It urges us to shift from division, hostility, heated arguments, fights and discord to a spirit of peace, understanding, harmony and cooperation. As a family, let's strive to cultivate unity, recognizing that it reflects the heart of God and brings blessing and favor to our lives.

Benefits of Growing in Unity:

Growing in unity strengthens our relationships, deepens our sense of belonging, and amplifies our impact in the world. It fosters a sense of community, mutual trust, friendship and camaraderie, enabling us to accomplish greater things together than we could ever achieve alone. Let's embrace the blessings that come from growing in unity, knowing that it glorifies God and advances His kingdom purposes.

Family Reflection:

Adult Perspective: Reflect on the importance of unity within your family, church, and community. How can you actively promote unity and reconciliation in relationships that may be strained or divided?

Child Perspective: Think about the value of teamwork and cooperation in your family and friendships. How can you contribute to unity by showing kindness, patience, and empathy towards others?

Tween Perspective: Consider the role of communication and understanding in fostering unity among peers and siblings. How can you resolve conflicts and build bridges of connection with those who may be different from you?

Teen Perspective: Reflect on the power of unity to bring about positive change in your school, church, or community. How can you collaborate with others to address issues of injustice, division, or inequality?

Transforming Our Mind:

Think about practical ways to promote unity in your family and community. How can you prioritize listening, empathy, and reconciliation in your interactions with others, seeking to build bridges of understanding and cooperation? The culture of the world influences people to look at others to compare, compete and criticize. We end up divided when we focus on our unique differences and our shortcomings. The culture of the world influences people to see differences in people as something wrong, weird or negative.

The culture of the world is the opposite of the culture of God's royal family. Our differences complement each other, helping us to live well with empathy. We lack nothing because of our diversity and intentionally living in unity as a collective powerful kingdom community that values and celebrates our unique purposeful divine designs and differences.

Additional Reading:

Explore these scriptures related to the theme. Read out loud, then share your thoughts about what the scriptures are saying and teaching us, especially about God, his values, Kingdom Culture and who we are as children of God:

> *Ephesians 4:2-3 (NASB)* - 'with all humility and gentleness, with patience, bearing with one another in love, being diligent to keep the unity of the Spirit in the bond of peace. '

> *Romans 12:16 (Passion Translation)* - "Live happily together in a spirit of harmony, and be as mindful of another's worth as you are your own. Don't live with a lofty mindset, thinking you are too important to serve others, but be willing to do menial tasks and identify with those who are humble minded. Don't be smug or even think for a moment that you know it all."

> Colossians 3:14 (ICB) - "Do all these things; but most important, love each other. Love is what holds you all together in perfect unity."

Family Declaration:

Together, let's declare: "We choose to grow in unity, celebrating our diversity and embracing one another with love and understanding. May our unity bring glory to God and blessings to our families, communities, and beyond."

Thanksgiving and Prayer for Guidance:

Thank You, Heavenly Father, for the gift of unity among believers. Heavenly Father, we come before you, asking for your help to grow in unity with one another. Help us to commit to growing in unity with our family, church, and community, embracing diversity and fostering harmony in all relationships. Help us, so we do not make what we personally like and prefer to form negative opinions or thoughts towards others. Help us to be open to learn from and about others and their experiences. We do not want to be limited in empathy, thinking our own experiences are the only experience and only way to do things and see things. Grant us the humility to lay aside our differences and the grace to embrace diversity, that we may reflect the beauty of your kingdom and cultivate kingdom culture here on earth. In Jesus' name, we pray. Amen.

Day 11: Embracing Humility

Welcome to Day 11 of our family devotional journey! Today, we are revisiting and focusing more closely on the virtue of humility and its transformative power in our relationships and attitudes. Let's explore how we can practically apply this truth to our lives.

Scripture: Philippians 2:3-4

> "Do nothing from selfishness or empty conceit, but with humility consider one another as more important than yourselves; do not merely look out for your own personal interests, but also for the interests of others." (NASB)

> 'Be free from pride-filled opinions, for they will only harm your cherished unity . Don't allow self-promotion to hide in your hearts, but in authentic humility put others first and view others as more important than yourselves. Abandon every display of selfishness. Possess a greater concern for what matters to others instead of your own interests. ' (TPT)

> "When you do things, do not let selfishness or pride be your guide. Be humble and give more honor to others than to yourselves. Do not be interested only in your own life, but be interested in the lives of others." (ICB)

Envisioning a Practical Connection:

Imagine a family where humility reigns, where each member esteems others above themselves and prioritizes the well-being of the whole. As adults, this means setting aside our own agendas and egos to serve and uplift those around us. For children, tweens, and teens, it's about learning to value others' perspectives and needs, practicing empathy and selflessness in all interactions.

Clarifying the Teaching:

This scripture reminds us to cultivate a spirit of humility, considering others' needs and interests as more important than our own. It urges us to shift from self-centeredness and pride to a posture of humility and servanthood. Being a parent can be a very humble job, wiping noses, changing diapers, and meeting a child's every need for years. Humble individuals genuinely care about the feelings and experiences of others. They treat everyone with courtesy and respect, regardless of their background or status.

As a family, let's embrace the humility modeled by Christ and seek to reflect His love and compassion in all we do.

Benefits of Embracing Humility:

Embracing humility fosters unity, harmony, and mutual respect within our families and communities. It breaks down barriers, fosters empathy, and promotes cooperation and understanding. Let's embrace the blessings that come from humbly serving and considering others, knowing that it reflects the heart of Christ and glorifies God.

Family Reflection: Share about new experiences both positive and challenging. Use this time to discuss things seen, heard or situations you or others are presently facing that relates to the virtue of humility.

Adult Perspective: Reflect on areas in your life where pride or self-centeredness may be hindering your relationships. How can you cultivate a spirit of humility and servanthood in your interactions with others?

Child Perspective: Think about a time when you put someone else's needs before your own. How did it feel to show kindness and consideration to others, and how can you continue to practice humility in your daily life?

Tween Perspective: Consider the importance of empathy and understanding in your friendships and family dynamics. How can you actively listen to others and show compassion and humility in your interactions?

Teen Perspective: Reflect on the role of humility in leadership and influence. How can you lead by example in your school or community by prioritizing the needs and interests of others above your own?

Transforming Our Mind:

Think about practical ways to cultivate humility in your family and community. How can you actively practice selflessness, empathy, and servanthood in your interactions with others, seeking to reflect the love of Christ in all you do?

Additional Reading:

Explore these scriptures related to the theme. Read out loud, then share your thoughts about what the scriptures are saying and teaching us, especially about God, his value, the Kingdom virtue of humility and who we are as children of God:

> *James 4:10 (Passion Translation)* - "Be willing to be made low before the Lord, and he will exalt you!"
>
> *Romans 12:16 (ICB)* - "Live together in peace with each other. Do not be proud, but make friends with those who seem unimportant. Do not think how smart you are."
>
> *Romans 12:16 (TPT)* - "Live happily together in a spirit of harmony, and be as mindful of another's worth as you are your own. Don't live with a lofty mind-set, thinking you are too important to serve others, but be willing to do menial tasks and identify with those who are humble minded. Don't be smug or even think for a moment that you know it all"
>
> *Proverbs 11:2 (TPT)* - "When you act with presumption, convinced that you're right, don't be surprised if you fall flat on your face! But humility leads to wisdom.

Family Declaration:

Together, let's declare: "We choose to embrace humility, considering others as important and serving with love and compassion. May our actions reflect the heart of Christ and bring glory to God."

Thanksgiving and Prayer for Guidance:

Thank You, Heavenly Father, for the example of humility demonstrated by Jesus Christ. Heavenly Father, we come before you, asking for your help to embrace humility in our hearts and attitudes. Teach us to consider others above our wants and to serve with love and compassion, just as Christ did. Help us to embrace humility in my relationships and interactions, considering others above ourselves and serving with love and compassion." In Jesus' name, we pray. Amen.

Day 12: Pursuing Forgiveness

Welcome to Day 12 of our family devotional journey! Today, we are revisiting the virtue of forgiveness, focusing on the transformative power it holds and the importance of extending grace to one another. Let's explore how we can practically apply this virtue in our lives.

Scripture: Matthew 18:21-22

> *Then Peter came up and said to Him, "Lord, how many times shall my brother sin against me and I still forgive him? Up to seven times?" Jesus said to him, "I do not say to you, up to seven times, but up to seventy-seven times. (NASB)*

> *'Later Peter approached Jesus and said, "How many times do I have to forgive my fellow believer who keeps offending me? Seven times?" Jesus answered, "Not seven times, Peter, but seventy times seven times! '(TPT)*

> *"Then Peter came to Jesus and asked, "Lord, when my brother sins against me, how many times must I forgive him? Should I forgive him as many as 7 times?" Jesus answered, "I tell you, you must forgive him more than 7 times. You must forgive him even if he does wrong to you 70 times 7". (ICB)*

Envisioning a Practical Connection:

Imagine a family where forgiveness flows freely, where hurts are healed, and relationships are restored. As adults, this means recognizing our own need for forgiveness and extending that same grace to those who have wronged us. For children, tweens, and teens, it's about learning to let go of grudges and offenses, choosing instead to forgive and reconcile with others.

Clarifying the Teaching:

This scripture reminds us to bear with one another and forgive as the Lord forgave us. It urges us to shift from harboring bitterness and resentment to extending mercy and grace. As a family, let's embrace the liberating power of forgiveness, knowing that it releases us from harmful mental bondage and restores harmony in our relationships.

Benefits of Pursuing Forgiveness:

Pursuing forgiveness brings healing, reconciliation, and freedom from the burden of unforgiveness. It opens the door to restored relationships, renewed trust, and greater intimacy in our relationship with God and others. Let's embrace the blessings that come from extending forgiveness, knowing that it reflects the heart of Christ, brings glory to God and health to our mind and body.

Family Reflection: Share about new experiences both positive and challenging. Use this time to discuss things seen, heard or situations you or others are presently facing that relate to the virtue of forgiveness.

Adult Perspective: Reflect on any unresolved conflicts or offenses in your relationships. How can you extend forgiveness and pursue reconciliation, following the example of Christ's forgiveness towards you?

Child Perspective: Think about a time when you felt hurt or wronged by someone. How did it feel to forgive them, and how can you choose forgiveness in future situations?

Tween Perspective: Consider the importance of forgiveness in maintaining healthy friendships and family dynamics. How can you practice forgiveness and reconciliation in your relationships with peers and siblings?

Teen Perspective: Reflect on the impact of forgiveness in your own life and relationships. How can you model forgiveness and extend grace to others, even when it's difficult or undeserved?

Transforming Our Mind:

Think about practical ways to pursue forgiveness in your family and community. How can you prioritize reconciliation, healing, and restoration in your interactions with others, seeking to reflect the love and forgiveness of Christ?

Additional Reading:

Explore these scriptures related to the theme. Read out loud, then share your thoughts about what the scriptures are saying and teaching us, especially about God, King Jesus and who we are as children of God:

> *Matthew 6:14-15 (TPT)* - "' And when you pray, make sure you forgive the faults of others so that your Father in heaven will also forgive you. But if you withhold forgiveness from others, your Father withholds forgiveness from you."
>
> *Psalms 86:5 (TPT)* 'Lord, you are so good to me, so kind in every way and ready to forgive, for your grace-fountain keeps overflowing, drenching all your devoted lovers who pray to you.'
>
> *Hebrews 8:12 (ICB)* 'I will forgive them for the wicked things they did. I will not remember their sins anymore."

Family commitment: Today I will intentionally...

Family Declaration:

Together, let's declare: "We choose to pursue forgiveness, extending grace and mercy to one another just as God and Christ forgave us. May our hearts be filled with love and compassion, leading to healing and restoration in our relationships."

Thanksgiving and Prayer for Guidance:

Thank You, Heavenly Father, for the gift of forgiveness made possible through Jesus Christ. Heavenly Father, we come before you, acknowledging our need for forgiveness and grace. Help us to extend the same mercy, grace and forgiveness to others that you have shown to us. Grant us the strength to let go of bitterness, grudges, irritation and resentment and pursue reconciliation, restored friendly relations, and healing in our relationships. Help our hearts to be filled with love and compassion. Let Your love and compassion lead to healing and restoration in our relationships. In Jesus' name, we pray. Amen.

Day 13: Cultivating Gratitude

Welcome to Day 13 of our family devotional journey! Today, we are revisiting the virtue of gratitude and focusing on the practice of cultivating gratitude in our hearts and lives. Let's explore how we can practically apply this truth to our daily walk with God.

Scripture: Ephesians 5:20

> 'always giving thanks for all things in the name of our Lord Jesus Christ to our God and Father; ' (NASB)

> 'Always give thanks to Father God for every person he brings into your life in the name of our Lord Jesus Christ.' (TPT)

> 'Always give thanks to God the Father for everything, in the name of our Lord Jesus Christ.' (ICB)

Envisioning a Practical Connection:

Imagine a family where gratitude abounds, where every blessing, big or small, is acknowledged and appreciated. As adults, this means developing a habit of gratitude, recognizing God's goodness in all circumstances and expressing thankfulness for His provision. For children, tweens, and teens, it's about learning to see the beauty in everyday moments and expressing gratitude for the gifts of family, friends, and experiences.

Clarifying the Teaching:

This scripture reminds us to give thanks in everything and for everything. We are reminded to recognize that gratitude is God's will for us in Christ Jesus. It urges us to shift from complaining and discontentment to a posture of gratitude and thanksgiving. As a family, let's embrace the practice of cultivating gratitude, knowing that it opens our hearts to God's blessings and transforms our perspective on life.

Benefits of Cultivating Gratitude:

Cultivating gratitude fosters a spirit of joy, contentment, and trust in God's provision. It shifts our focus from what we lack to what we have, fostering a sense of abundance and appreciation for the goodness of God. Let's embrace the blessings that come from cultivating gratitude, knowing that it deepens our relationship with God and enriches our lives in countless ways. Our gratitude transforms our perspective and influences those around us. Our gratitude affects our attitude, increases positive thoughts, makes you feel happier and impacts others in your environments.

Family Reflection: Share about new experiences both positive and challenging. Use this time to discuss things seen, heard or situations you or others are presently facing that relate to the virtue of gratitude.

Adult Perspective: Reflect on the blessings in your life, both big and small, and consider how cultivating gratitude can transform your perspective on challenges and difficulties. How can you cultivate a habit of thankfulness in your daily walk with God?

Child Perspective: Think about something you're thankful for today, whether it's a favorite toy, a special friend, or a delicious meal. How does expressing gratitude make you feel, and how can you practice thankfulness in your daily life?

Tween Perspective: Consider the importance of gratitude in cultivating a positive outlook and mindset. How can you express thankfulness for the people, opportunities, and experiences that enrich your life?

Teen Perspective: Reflect on the role of gratitude in navigating the ups and downs of adolescence. How can you cultivate a heart of thankfulness amidst the challenges and uncertainties you may face?

Transforming Our Mind:

Think about practical ways to cultivate gratitude in your family and community. How can you prioritize thankfulness in your interactions with others, seeking to express appreciation and acknowledge God's goodness in all circumstances?

Additional Reading:

Explore these scriptures related to the theme. Read out loud, then share your thoughts about what the scriptures are saying and teaching us, especially about God, Jesus Christ, the virtue of gratitude/thankfulness and who we are as children of God:

Psalm 100:4 (NASB) - "Enter His gates with thanksgiving and His courts with praise. Give thanks to Him, bless His name."

Colossians 3:15, 17 (Passion Translation) - "Let your heart be always guided by the peace of the Anointed One, who called you to peace as part of his one body. And always be thankful. Let every activity of your lives and every word that comes from your lips be drenched with the beauty of our Lord Jesus, the Anointed One. And bring your constant praise to God the Father because of what Christ has done for you!"

Psalm 107:1 (ICB) - "Thank the Lord because he is good. His love continues forever."

1 Thessalonians 5:18 "Give thanks whatever happens. That is what God wants for you in Christ Jesus." (ICB)

Psalms 28:7 (NASB) - 'The Lord is my strength and my shield; My heart trusts in Him, and I am helped; Therefore my heart triumphs, And with my song I shall thank Him. '

Family commitment: Today I will intentionally...

Family Declaration:

Together, let's declare: "We choose to cultivate gratitude, giving thanks in everything and acknowledging God's goodness in our lives. May our hearts overflow with thankfulness, reflecting the joy and abundance found in Christ Jesus."

Thanksgiving and Prayer for Guidance:

Thank You, Heavenly Father, for the countless blessings You have bestowed upon us. Heavenly Father, we come before you with grateful hearts, acknowledging Your goodness and faithfulness in our lives. Help us to cultivate a spirit of gratitude, recognizing Your blessings and expressing thankfulness in all circumstances. We acknowledge Your goodness in our life. We thank You for filling our hearts with joy and thankfulness for Your abundant provision. In Jesus' name, we pray. Amen.

Day 14: Seeking God's Wisdom

Welcome to Day 14 of our family devotional journey! Today, we are revisiting and focusing more closely on the importance of seeking God's wisdom in every aspect of our lives. Let's explore how we can practically apply this truth to grow in understanding and discernment.

Scriptures: James 1:5-7

'But if any of you lacks wisdom, let him ask of God, who gives to all generously and without reproach, and it will be given to him. But he must ask in faith without any doubting, for the one who doubts is like the surf of the sea, driven and tossed by the wind. For that person ought not to expect that he will receive anything from the Lord, '(NASB)

"And if anyone longs to be wise, ask God for wisdom and he will give it! He won't see your lack of wisdom as an opportunity to scold you over your failures but he will overwhelm your failures with his generous grace. Just make sure you ask empowered by confident faith without doubting that you will receive. For the ambivalent person believes one minute and doubts the next. Being undecided makes you become like the rough seas driven and tossed by the wind. You're up one minute and tossed down the next. When you are half-hearted and wavering it leaves you unstable. Can you really expect to receive anything from the Lord when you're in that condition? When you are half-hearted and wavering it leaves you unstable. Can you really expect to receive anything from the Lord when you're in that condition? '(TPT)

'"But if any of you needs wisdom, you should ask God for it. God is generous. He enjoys giving to all people, so God will give you wisdom. But when you ask God, you must believe. Do not doubt God. Anyone who doubts is like a wave in the sea. The wind blows the wave up and down. He who doubts is thinking two different things at the same time. He cannot decide about anything he does. A person like that should not think that he will receive anything from the Lord. He who doubts is thinking two different things at the same time. He cannot decide about anything he does. A person like that should not think that he will receive anything from the Lord.' (ICB)

Envisioning a Practical Connection:

Imagine a family where wisdom guides every decision, where God's insights illuminate the path forward. As adults, this means acknowledging our limitations and seeking God's guidance in our choices, relationships, and endeavors. For children, tweens, and teens, it's about learning to rely on God's wisdom in navigating challenges, making decisions, and seeking direction for the future.

Clarifying the Teaching:

These scriptures remind us that God is the ultimate source of wisdom, and He generously gives wisdom to those who ask in faith. It urges us to shift from relying solely on our own understanding to trusting in God's infinite wisdom and insight. As a family, let's embrace the practice of seeking God's wisdom in all we do, knowing that it leads to discernment, clarity, and alignment with His will.

Benefits of Seeking God's Wisdom:

Seeking God's wisdom empowers us to make wise choices, navigate challenges, and discern His perfect will for our lives. It provides clarity in the midst of confusion, direction in times of uncertainty, and peace amidst chaos. Let's embrace the blessings that come from seeking God's wisdom, knowing that it leads to abundant life and fulfillment in Christ.

Family Reflection:

Adult Perspective: Reflect on areas in your life where you need God's wisdom and guidance. How can you cultivate a habit of seeking His wisdom through prayer, Scripture, and wise counsel from others?

Child Perspective: Think about a decision you need to make, whether it's choosing between right and wrong or deciding what to do with your free time. How can you seek God's wisdom and guidance in making wise choices?

Tween Perspective: Consider the importance of seeking God's wisdom in friendships, schoolwork, and extracurricular activities. How can you rely on His guidance to navigate peer pressure, academic challenges, and social dynamics?

Teen Perspective: Reflect on the significance of seeking God's wisdom in planning for the future, making major life decisions, and pursuing your passions and dreams. How can you trust God's guidance and timing in shaping your identity and purpose?

Transforming Our Mind:

Think about practical ways to seek God's wisdom in your family and community. How can you prioritize prayer, Scripture reading, and seeking wise counsel from others in decision-making and discernment?

Additional Reading:

Explore these scriptures related to the theme. Read out loud, then share your thoughts about what the scriptures are saying and teaching us, especially about God and who we are as children of God:

Proverbs 3:5-7 (ICB) - '"Trust the Lord with all your heart. Don't depend on your own understanding. Remember the Lord in everything you do. And he will give you success. Don't depend on your own wisdom. Respect the Lord and refuse to do wrong.'

1 Kings 4:29-30 (NASB) 'Now God gave Solomon wisdom and very great discernment and breadth of mind, like the sand that is on the seashore. Solomon's wisdom surpassed the wisdom of all the people of the east and all the wisdom of Egypt.

Family Declaration:

Together, let's declare: "We choose to seek God's wisdom in all we do, trusting in His guidance and understanding. May His wisdom illuminate our path and lead us into His perfect will for our lives."

Thanksgiving and Prayer for Guidance:

Thank You, Heavenly Father, for the gift of Your wisdom, freely given to all who ask in faith. Heavenly Father, we come before you, acknowledging our need for Your wisdom and guidance in every aspect of our lives. Grant us the humility to seek Your wisdom with sincerity and faith, trusting that You will generously provide all we need. Your wisdom leads us into Your perfect will for our lives." In Jesus' name, we pray. Amen.

Day 15: Trusting in God's Provision

Welcome to Day 15 of our family devotional journey! Today, we focus on trusting in God's provision for all our needs. Let's explore how we can practically apply this truth to our lives.

Scriptures: Matthew 6:31-33

> "Do not worry then, saying, 'What will we eat?' or 'What will we drink?' or 'What will we wear for clothing?' For the Gentiles eagerly seek all these things; for your heavenly Father knows that you need all these things. But seek first His kingdom and His righteousness, and all these things will be added to you." (NASB)

> "'So then, forsake your worries! Why would you say, 'What will we eat?' or 'What will we drink?' or 'What will we wear?' For that is what the unbelievers chase after. Doesn't your heavenly Father already know the things your bodies require? "So above all, constantly seek God's kingdom and his righteousness, then all these less important things will be given to you abundantly." (TPT)

> "Don't worry and say, 'What will we eat?' or 'What will we drink?' or 'What will we wear?' All the people who don't know God keep trying to get these things. And your Father in heaven knows that you need them. The thing you should want most is God's kingdom and doing what God wants. Then all these other things you need will be given to you." (ICB)

Envisioning a Practical Connection:

Imagine a family where worries about material needs are replaced with confidence in God's faithfulness. As adults, this means prioritizing seeking God's kingdom and righteousness above worldly concerns and possessions, trusting that He will provide for our needs. For children, tweens, and teens, it's about learning to trust God's provision for everyday needs and embracing a lifestyle of faith over fear.

Clarifying the Teaching:

This scripture reminds us of God's loving care and provision for His children. It urges us to shift from anxious striving to confident reliance on God's faithfulness. As a family, let's embrace the truth that God knows our needs and is faithful to provide when we seek Him first.

Benefits of Trusting in God's Provision:

Trusting in God's provision brings peace, contentment, and freedom from worry. It allows us to live with open hands, knowing that our heavenly Father is faithful to provide for all our needs. God provides for us through others. God works in us and through us for each other. He wants us to receive, accept and acknowledge his provisions. People will offer to help and assist, allow them to be the hand of God, receive his goodness. At times we may feel compelled to help or assist others. This is how God works within us. Let's embrace the blessings that come from trusting in God's provision, knowing that He is our ultimate source of security and provision.

Family Reflection:

Adult Perspective: Reflect on areas of worry or anxiety in your life related to finances or material needs. How can you surrender these concerns to God and trust in His provision, seeking first His kingdom and righteousness?

Child Perspective: Think about a time when you felt worried about something you needed. How did God provide for you, and how can you trust Him to meet your needs in the future?

Tween Perspective: Consider the importance of prioritizing God's kingdom above worldly concerns. How can you seek first His kingdom and righteousness in your everyday life, trusting that He will provide for all your needs?

Teen Perspective: Reflect on the temptation to worry about the future and material needs. How can you cultivate a mindset of trust and reliance on God's provision, knowing that He is faithful to provide when we seek Him first?

Transforming Our Mind:

Think about practical ways to trust in God's provision in your family and community. How can you prioritize seeking God's kingdom and righteousness above worldly concerns, trusting that He will provide for all your needs according to His riches in glory?

Additional Reading:

Explore these scriptures related to the theme. Read out loud, then share your thoughts about what the scriptures are saying and teaching us, especially about God and who we are as children of God:

> *Philippians 4:19 (NASB)* - "And my God will supply all your needs according to His riches in glory in Christ Jesus."

> *Psalm 23:1 (Passion Translation)* - "The Lord is my best friend and my shepherd. I always have more than enough."

> *Psalm 34:10 (NASB)* - "The young lions do lack and suffer hunger; but they who seek the Lord shall not be in want of any good thing."

> *Philipians 4:6 (ICB)* - "'Do not worry about anything. But pray and ask God for everything you need. And when you pray, always give thanks. '

Family commitment: Today I will intentionally...

Family Declaration:

Together, let's declare: "We choose to trust in God's provision, seeking first His kingdom and righteousness. May our hearts be free from worry as we rely on His faithfulness to provide for all our needs."

Thanksgiving and Prayer for Guidance:

Thank You, Heavenly Father, for Your faithful provision in our lives. Heavenly Father, we come before you, acknowledging our tendency to worry about material needs and provision. Help us to trust in Your faithfulness and seek first Your kingdom and righteousness, knowing that You will provide for all our needs according to Your riches in glory. In Jesus' name, we pray. Amen.

Day 16: Walking in Faith

Welcome to Day 16 of our family devotional journey! Today, we delve into the concept of faith and its transformative power in our lives. Let's explore how we can practically apply this truth to our daily walk with God.

Scripture: Hebrews 11:1

> "Now faith is the assurance of things hoped for, the conviction of things not seen." (NASB)

> 'Now faith brings our hopes into reality and becomes the foundation needed to acquire the things we long for. It is all the evidence required to prove what is still unseen. ' (TPT)

> "Faith means being sure of the things we hope for. And faith means knowing that something is real even if we do not see it." (ICB)

Envisioning a Practical Connection:

Imagine a family where faith serves as the foundation for every decision and action, where hope abounds, and prayers are answered. As adults, this means anchoring our lives in the promises of God, trusting Him even when circumstances seem uncertain. For children, tweens, and teens, it's about learning about God, his words, his love and character. It's about learning to trust God's promises, plan and purpose, believing in His faithfulness to fulfill His promises and keep his word.

Clarifying the Teaching:

This scripture reminds us that faith is the assurance of things hoped for and the conviction of things not seen. It urges us to shift from doubt and fear to a posture of trust and confidence in God's faithfulness. As a family, let's embrace the power of faith, knowing that it moves mountains and unlocks the miraculous in our lives.

Benefits of Walking in Faith:

Walking in faith opens the door to God's supernatural provision, protection, and guidance in our lives. It strengthens our relationship with Him, deepens our intimacy with the Father, and empowers us to overcome obstacles and challenges. Let's embrace the blessings that come from walking in faith, knowing that it pleases God and brings glory to His name. Walking in faith builds our *GODfindence,* our belief, trust and confidence in God, his word, his power, promises, love and provision.

Family Reflection:

Adult Perspective: Reflect on moments in your life where God has demonstrated His faithfulness and provision. How can you strengthen your faith and trust in God's promises, especially during times of uncertainty or difficulty?

Child Perspective: Think about a time when you prayed and saw God answer your prayers. How did it feel to trust God and see His faithfulness in action, and how can you continue to walk in faith in your daily life?

Tween Perspective: Consider the role of faith in facing challenges and uncertainties in your life. How can you cultivate a deeper trust in God and His promises, believing that He is always with you and for you?

Teen Perspective: Reflect on the impact of faith on your relationship with God and others. How can you actively walk in faith, trusting God's plan and purpose for your life and living with confidence in His unfailing love and provision?

Transforming Our Mind:

Think about practical ways to walk in faith in your family and community. How can you prioritize prayer, Scripture reading to embrace and memorize God's truths, demonstrating obedience to God's Word, cultivating a heart of trust and confidence in His promises?

Additional Reading:

Explore these scriptures related to the theme. Read out loud, then share your thoughts about what the scriptures are saying and teaching us, especially about God and who we are as children of God:

Mark 11:24 (NASB) - "Therefore I say to you, all things for which you pray and ask, believe that you have received them, and they will be granted you."

Matthew 17:20 (Passion Translation) - "He told them, 'It was because of your lack of faith. I promise you, if you have faith inside of you no bigger than the size of a small mustard seed, you can say to this mountain, 'Move away from here and go over there,' and you will see it move!'"

Romans 10:17 (NASB) - "So faith comes from hearing, and hearing by the word of Christ."

Romans 10:17 (ICB) - "So faith comes from hearing the Good News. And people hear the Good News when someone tells them about Christ."

Family commitment: Today I will intentionally...

Family Declaration:

Together, let's declare: "We choose to walk in faith, trusting God's promises and believing in His faithfulness to fulfill His plans for our lives. May our lives be a testimony of His goodness and grace, inspiring others to trust in Him."

Thanksgiving and Prayer for Guidance:

Thank You, Heavenly Father, for the gift of faith that enables us to trust in Your unfailing love and promises. Heavenly Father, we come before you, acknowledging our need for faith and trust in Your unfailing love, promises and faithfulness. Strengthen our faith, Lord, and help us to walk confidently in Your promises, knowing that You are always with us and for us. Help us to walk in faith, trusting in Your goodness and faithfulness to fulfill Your plans for our lives. Your promises are our assurance, and Your love is our strength. Because of who You are, we thank you and have GODfidence in You" In Jesus' name, we pray. Amen.

Day 17: Seeking Wisdom

Welcome to Day 17 of our family devotional journey! Today, we are revisiting the value of wisdom and delve into the importance and benefits of seeking wisdom from God. Let's explore how we can practically apply this truth to our lives.

Scripture: James 3:17

"But the wisdom from above is first pure, then peaceable, gentle, reasonable, full of mercy and good fruits, unwavering, without hypocrisy." (NASB)

'But the wisdom from above is always pure, filled with peace, considerate and teachable. It is filled with love and never displays prejudice or hypocrisy in any form '(TPT)

"But the wisdom that comes from God is like this: First, it is pure. Then it is also peaceful, gentle, and easy to please. This wisdom is always ready to help those who are troubled and to do good for others. This wisdom is always fair and honest." (ICB)

Envisioning a Practical Connection:

Imagine a family where wisdom guides every decision and action, where each member seeks God's guidance in all things. As adults, this means acknowledging our need for wisdom and turning to God in prayer for discernment and direction. For children, tweens, and teens, it's about learning to seek God's wisdom in school, friendships, and future plans.

Clarifying the Teaching:

This scripture reminds us that God is the source of all wisdom, and He generously gives wisdom to those who ask. It urges us to recognize that true wisdom comes from God alone. True wisdom is God's way of doing things. As a family, let's embrace the practice of seeking wisdom from God, knowing that it leads to discernment, clarity, and understanding in all areas of life.

Benefits of Seeking Wisdom:

Seeking wisdom from God enables us to make wise decisions, navigate challenges, and walk in alignment with His will. It brings clarity to confusing situations, peace when there is uncertainty, and direction for the future. Let's embrace the blessings that come from seeking wisdom, knowing that it leads to a life of reflective intentional righteous decisions, purpose and fulfillment.

Family Reflection: Share about new experiences both positive and challenging. Use this time to discuss things seen, heard or situations you or others are presently facing that relate to the value and virtue of seeking God's wisdom.

Adult Perspective: Reflect on a recent decision or challenge you faced and consider how seeking God's wisdom could have impacted the outcome. How can you prioritize seeking wisdom in all areas of your life, trusting in God's guidance and direction?

Child Perspective: Think about a decision you have to make at school or with friends. How can you seek God's wisdom in this situation, trusting that He will give you the understanding and clarity you need?

Tween Perspective: Consider the importance of seeking God's wisdom as you navigate the challenges of adolescence. How can you make seeking wisdom a priority in your daily life, trusting in God's guidance for your future?

Teen Perspective: Reflect on the significance of seeking wisdom as you make decisions about your education, career, and relationships. How can you seek God's wisdom in these important areas of your life, trusting in His perfect plan for you?

Transforming Our Mind:

Think about practical ways to seek wisdom from God in your family and community. How can you prioritize prayer, scripture reading, and seeking counsel from wise mentors, knowing that God generously gives wisdom to all who ask? Be aware and mindful that worldly wisdom is different from Godly wisdom.

Additional Reading:

Explore these scriptures related to the theme. Read out loud, then share your thoughts about what the scriptures are saying and teaching us, especially about God, the value and benefits of seeking God's wisdom and who we are as children of God:

Proverbs 12:15 (NASB) - 'The way of a fool is right in his own eyes, But a person who listens to advice is wise.

Proverbs 3:13-14 (Passion Translation) - "'Blessings pour over the ones who find wisdom, for they have obtained living-understanding. As wisdom increases, a great treasure is imparted, greater than many bars of refined gold.'"

Proverbs 2:6 (TPT) - "'Wisdom is a gift from a generous God, and every word he speaks is full of revelation and becomes a fountain of understanding within you. '

Psalm 119:105 (ICB) - "Your word is like a lamp for my feet and a light for my way.

Psalms 119:105 (TPT) -'Truth's shining light guides me in my choices and decisions; the revelation of your Word makes my pathway clear.'

Family commitment: Today I will intentionally...

Family Declaration:

Together, let's declare: "We choose to seek wisdom from God in all things, trusting in His guidance and direction for our lives. May His wisdom lead us to discernment, clarity, and understanding in every decision we make."

Thanksgiving and Prayer for guidance:

Heavenly Father, we come before you, acknowledging our need for wisdom in all areas of our lives. Grant us discernment and understanding as we seek Your guidance and direction. Help us to trust in Your wisdom, knowing that You give generously to all who ask and believe.

Thank You, Heavenly Father, for the gift of wisdom available to us through Your Word, Your Spirit and righteous counsel from mature mentors and those with Your gained wisdom. Help us to seek wisdom from You God in all things, trusting in Your guidance and direction for our lives. Thank you for your love and generosity of wisdom because Your wisdom leads us to discernment, clarity, and understanding in every decision we make." In Jesus' name, we pray. Amen.

Day 18: Cultivating Patience

Welcome to Day 18 of our family devotional journey! Today, we explore the virtue of patience and its transformative power in our relationships and attitudes. Let's delve into how we can practically apply this truth to our lives.

Scriptures: James 1:19-20

"This you know, my beloved brethren. But everyone must be quick to hear, slow to speak and slow to anger; for the anger of man does not achieve the righteousness of God." (NASB)

'My dearest brothers and sisters, take this to heart: Be quick to listen, but slow to speak. And be slow to become angry, for human anger is never a legitimate tool to promote God's righteous purpose. ' (TPT)

"My dear brothers, always be willing to listen and slow to speak. Do not become angry easily. Anger will not help you live a good life as God wants." (ICB)

Envisioning a Practical Connection:

Imagine a family where patience abounds, where misunderstandings or conflicts are resolved with patience to understand one another and learn from each other with grace, and where love prevails in every interaction. As adults, this means cultivating patience in our communication and interactions with others, seeking to understand before reacting. For children, tweens, and teens, it's about learning to pause before responding, listening with empathy, and choosing patience in moments of frustration.

Clarifying the Teaching:

This scripture reminds us of the importance of patience in our relationships. It urges us to shift from impulsiveness and quick anger to a posture of patience and understanding. As a family, let's embrace the practice of cultivating patience, knowing that it fosters harmony, empathy, and grace in all our interactions.

Benefits of Cultivating Patience:

Cultivating patience leads to deeper understanding, stronger relationships, and greater peace in our lives. It enables us to respond with grace and wisdom, even in the face of challenging circumstances. When we are not patient, we tend to react without thinking or considering the lasting outcomes of our own behavior and words. Let's embrace the blessings that come from cultivating patience, knowing that it reflects the character of Christ and brings glory to God.

Family Reflection:

Adult Perspective: Reflect on moments when impatience or anger hindered your relationships. How can you cultivate patience in your interactions with others, seeking to understand before reacting, and extending grace and empathy in all circumstances?

Child Perspective: Think about a time when you felt impatient or frustrated with a sibling or friend. How did it feel, and how could choosing patience have changed the outcome of the situation?

Tween Perspective: Consider the importance of patience in resolving conflicts and misunderstandings with peers and family members. How can you cultivate patience in your interactions, seeking to listen and understand before reacting?

Teen Perspective: Reflect on the impact of patience in your relationships and communication with others. How can you cultivate patience, even in moments of frustration or disagreement, seeking to respond with grace and empathy?

Transforming Our Mind:

Think about practical ways to cultivate patience in your family and community. How can you prioritize active listening, empathy, and grace in your interactions with others, seeking to reflect the patience and love of Christ?

Additional Reading:

Explore these scriptures related to the theme. Read out loud, then share your thoughts about what the scriptures are saying and teaching us, especially about God and who we are as children of God:

> *1 Corinthians 13:4 (TPT)* - 'Love is large and incredibly patient. Love is gentle and consistently kind to all. It refuses to be jealous when blessing comes to someone else . Love does not brag about one's achievements nor inflate its own importance. '

> *Ephesians 4:2 (TPT)* - "With tender humility and quiet patience, always demonstrate gentleness and generous love toward one another, especially toward those who may try your patience."

> *Colossians 3:12 (TPT)* - '"You are always and dearly loved by God! So robe yourself with virtues of God , since you have been divinely chosen to be holy. Be merciful as you endeavor to understand others, and be compassionate, showing kindness toward all. Be gentle and humble, unoffendable in your patience with others. '

> *Galatians 5:22-23, 25 (ICB)* - "But the Spirit gives love, joy, peace, patience, kindness, goodness, faithfulness, gentleness, self-control. There is no law that says these things are wrong. If we live by the Spirit, let us also walk by the Spirit.

Family commitment: Today I will intentionally...

Family Declaration:

Together, let's declare: "We choose to cultivate patience in our relationships and interactions, seeking to understand before reacting and extending grace and empathy to others. May our patience foster harmony, understanding, and love in our family and community."

Thanksgiving and Prayer for Guidance:

Thank You, Heavenly Father, for Your patience and grace towards us. Heavenly Father, we come before you, acknowledging our need for patience in our relationships and interactions. Grant us the grace to be quick to listen, slow to speak, and slow to anger, that we may reflect Your patience and love to those around us. Help us to cultivate patience in our relationships, seeking to understand before reacting and extending grace and empathy to others. May our patience foster and encourage harmony, understanding, and love in our family and community." In Jesus' name, we pray. Amen.

Day 19: Practicing Kindness

Welcome to Day 19 of our family devotional journey! Today, we explore the transformative power of kindness and its profound impact on our relationships and attitudes. Let's delve into how we can practically apply this truth to our lives.

Scripture: Ephesians 4:32

"Be kind to one another, tender-hearted, forgiving each other, just as God in Christ also has forgiven you."(NASB)

'But instead be kind and affectionate toward one another. Has God graciously forgiven you? Then graciously forgive one another in the depths of Christ's love.' (TPT)

"Be kind and loving to each other. Forgive each other just as God forgave you in Christ." (ICB)

Envisioning a Practical Connection:

Imagine a family where kindness reigns supreme, where every interaction is marked by compassion, generosity, and grace. As adults, this means making a conscious effort to extend kindness in our words and actions, showing empathy and understanding to those around us. For children, tweens, and teens, it's about learning to look for opportunities to show kindness to others, whether it's through simple acts of service, words of encouragement, or expressions of love.

Clarifying the Teaching:

This scripture reminds us of the importance of kindness in our relationships. It urges us to shift from indifference or self-centeredness to a posture of kindness, friendliness, consideration and compassion. As a family, let's embrace the practice of cultivating kindness, knowing that it reflects the heart of Christ and brings healing and restoration to our relationships.

Benefits of Practicing Kindness:

Practicing kindness fosters unity, empathy, and goodwill in our families and communities. It builds bridges, fosters understanding, and brings hope to those in need. Kindness extends love to others. Being kind to ourselves in words and deeds fosters love towards ourselves. Let's embrace the blessings that come from practicing kindness, knowing that it reflects the character of Christ and glorifies God.

Family Reflection:

Adult Perspective: Reflect on moments when kindness made a difference in your relationships. How can you cultivate a spirit of kindness in your interactions with others, seeking to extend grace and compassion in all circumstances?

Child Perspective: Think about a time when someone showed kindness to you. How did it make you feel, and how can you pay it forward by showing kindness to others?

Tween Perspective: Consider the importance of kindness in building friendships and resolving conflicts. How can you actively practice kindness in your interactions with peers and family members?

Teen Perspective: Reflect on the impact of kindness in your school or community. How can you be intentional about showing kindness to those around you, seeking to make a positive difference in the lives of others?

Transforming Our Mind:

Think about practical ways to practice kindness in your family and community. How can you prioritize acts of service, words of encouragement, and expressions of love, knowing that kindness has the power to transform hearts and bring healing and restoration?

Additional Reading:

Explore these scriptures related to the theme. Read out loud, then share your thoughts about what the scriptures are saying and teaching us, especially about God , the virtue of kindness and who we are as children of God:

Luke 6:31 (NASB) - "Treat others the same way you want them to treat you."

Proverbs 11:25 (Passion Translation) - "The one who blesses others is abundantly blessed; those who help others are helped."

Matthew 7:12 (TPT) - *"'In everything you do, be careful to treat others in the same way you'd want them to treat you, for that is the essence of all the teachings of the Law and the Prophets. '*

Family commitment: Today I will intentionally...

Family Declaration:

Together, let's declare: "We choose to practice kindness in our relationships and interactions, showing compassion and grace to those around us. May our acts of kindness reflect the love of Christ and bring healing and restoration to our family and community."

Thanksgiving and Prayer for Guidance:

Thank You, Heavenly Father, for the gift of kindness demonstrated through Christ's sacrificial love. Heavenly Father, we come before you, asking for the grace to practice kindness in our relationships and interactions. Help us to be tender-hearted, friendly and compassionate, showing empathy and understanding to those around us, just as You have shown kindness to us. Help our acts of kindness reflect the love of Christ and bring healing and restoration to our family and community." In Jesus' name, we pray. Amen.

Day 20: Embracing Humility

Welcome to Day 20 of our family devotional journey! Today, we are revisiting the value and virtue of humility. We will explore the transformative virtue of humility and its profound benefits and impact on our relationships and attitudes. Let's delve into how we can practically apply this truth to our lives.

Scriptures: Philippians 2:3-4

"Do nothing from selfishness or empty conceit, but with humility consider one another as more important than yourselves; do not merely look out for your own personal interests, but also for the interests of others."(NASB)

'Be free from pride-filled opinions, for they will only harm your cherished unity . Don't allow self-promotion to hide in your hearts, but in authentic humility put others first and view others as more important than yourselves. Abandon every display of selfishness. Possess a greater concern for what matters to others instead of your own interests.' (TPT)

"When you do things, do not let selfishness or pride be your guide. Be humble and give more honor to others than to yourselves. Do not be interested only in your own life, but be interested in the lives of others." (ICB)

Envisioning a Practical Connection:

Imagine a family where humility reigns supreme, where each member considers others' needs before their own and where pride is replaced with genuine humility. As adults, this means setting aside our ego and selfish desires, choosing instead to serve and uplift those around us. For children, tweens, and teens, it's about learning to value others' perspectives and feelings, recognizing the importance of putting others first.

Clarifying the Teaching:

This scripture reminds us of the importance of humility in our interactions with others. It urges us to shift from self-centeredness and pride to a posture of humility and servanthood. As a family, let's embrace the practice of embracing humility, knowing that it fosters unity, empathy, and love in our relationships.

Benefits of Embracing Humility:

Embracing humility leads to deeper relationships, greater empathy, and genuine love for others. It fosters unity and cooperation within our families and communities, breaking down barriers and building bridges of understanding. Let's embrace the blessings that come from embracing humility, knowing that it reflects the heart of Christ and brings glory to God.

Family Reflection:

Adult Perspective: Reflect on moments when pride or selfishness hindered your relationships. How can you cultivate a spirit of humility in your interactions with others, seeking to serve and uplift those around you?

Child Perspective: Think about a time when you felt proud or self-centered. How did it affect your relationships with others, and how can you practice humility by considering others' needs before your own?

Tween Perspective: Consider the importance of humility in building friendships and resolving conflicts. How can you cultivate humility in your interactions with peers and family members, seeking to value others' perspectives and feelings?

Teen Perspective: Reflect on the impact of humility in your school or community. How can you be intentional about embracing humility, recognizing the value of serving and uplifting those around you?

Transforming Our Mind:

Think about practical ways to embrace humility in your family and community. How can you prioritize serving others, valuing their perspectives and feelings, and putting their needs before your own, knowing that humility has the power to transform hearts and build unity?

Additional Reading:

Explore these scriptures related to the theme. Read out loud, then share your thoughts about what the scriptures are saying and teaching us, especially about God, Kingdom culture and who we are as children of God:

Matthew 23:12 (NASB) - "Whoever exalts himself shall be humbled; and whoever humbles himself shall be exalted."

Psalms 25:9 (NASB) - "He leads the humble in justice, And He teaches the humble His way.

Psalms 149:4 (TPT) - "For he enjoys his faithful lovers. He adorns the humble with his beauty, and he loves to give them victory.

Proverbs 22:4 (NASB) - "The reward of humility *and* the fear of the L○○○
Are riches, honor, and life.

Ephesians 4:2-6 (ICB) - "Always be humble and gentle. Be patient and accept each other with love. You are joined together with peace through the Spirit. Do all you can to continue together in this way. Let peace hold you together. There is one body and one Spirit. And God called you to have one hope. There is one Lord, one faith, and one baptism. There is one God and Father of everything. He rules everything. He is everywhere and in everything."

Family commitment: Today I will intentionally...

Family Declaration:

Together, let's declare: "We choose to embrace humility in our relationships and interactions, considering others as more important than ourselves and seeking to serve and uplift those around us. May our humility foster unity, empathy, and love in our family and community."

Thanksgiving and Prayer for Guidance:

Thank You, Heavenly Father, for the example of humility demonstrated through Christ's sacrificial love. Heavenly Father, we come before you, asking for the grace to embrace humility in our relationships and interactions. Help us to embrace humility in our relationships, considering the needs of others as more important than our interest and seeking to serve and uplift those around us. Help us to set aside our pride and selfish desires and interest, choosing instead to serve and uplift those around us, just as Christ humbly served us. In Jesus' name, we pray. Amen.

Day 21: Fostering Forgiveness

Welcome to Day 21 of our family devotional journey! Today, we revisit the profound virtue and practice of forgiveness and explore its transformative power in our relationships and attitudes. Let's delve into how we can practically apply this virtuous truth to our lives.

Scripture: Proverbs 17:9

> "Bearing with one another, and forgiving each other, whoever has a complaint against anyone; just as the Lord forgave you, so also should you forgive." (NASB)

> 'Tolerate the weaknesses of those in the family of faith, forgiving one another in the same way you have been graciously forgiven by Jesus Christ. If you find fault with someone, release this same gift of forgiveness to them. ' (TPT)

> "Do not be angry with each other, but forgive each other. If someone does wrong to you, then forgive him. Forgive each other because the Lord forgave you." (ICB)

Envisioning a Practical Connection:

Imagine a family where forgiveness flows freely, where grievances are addressed with grace and reconciliation is sought with sincerity. As adults, this means cultivating a heart of forgiveness, choosing to release resentment, grudges and extend grace to those who have wronged us. For children, tweens, and teens, it's about learning to let go of hurt and bitterness, embracing forgiveness as a pathway to healing and restoration in relationships.

Clarifying the Teaching:

This scripture reminds us of the importance of forgiveness in our relationships. It urges us to shift from holding onto grudges and resentment to a posture of grace and reconciliation. As a family, let's embrace the practice of fostering forgiveness, knowing that it leads to freedom, healing, and unity in our relationships.

Benefits of Fostering Forgiveness:

Fostering forgiveness leads to reconciliation, healing, and restored relationships. It releases the burden of resentment and bitterness, freeing us to experience peace and joy in our interactions with others. Let's embrace the blessings that come from fostering forgiveness, knowing that it reflects the heart of Christ and brings glory to God.

Family Reflection:

Adult Perspective: Reflect on moments when forgiveness brought healing and restoration in your relationships. How can you cultivate a spirit of forgiveness in your interactions with others, choosing to extend grace and reconciliation as Christ has done for us?

Child Perspective: Think about a time when you forgave someone who hurt you. How did it feel, and how can you practice forgiveness by choosing to let go of hurt and extend grace to others?

Tween Perspective: Consider the importance of forgiveness in resolving conflicts and restoring friendships. How can you cultivate a heart of forgiveness in your interactions with peers and family members, seeking reconciliation and healing in relationships?

Teen Perspective: Reflect on the impact of forgiveness in your school or community. How can you be intentional about fostering forgiveness, choosing to release resentment and bitterness and extend grace and reconciliation to those who have wronged you?

Transforming Our Mind:

Think about practical ways to foster forgiveness in your family and community. How can you prioritize addressing grievances with grace, seeking reconciliation and healing in relationships, and extending forgiveness as Christ has done for us?

Additional Reading:

Explore these scriptures related to the theme. Read out loud, then share your thoughts about what the scriptures are saying and teaching us, especially about God and who we are as children of God:

Matthew 6:14-15 (NASB) - "For if you forgive others for their transgressions, your heavenly Father will also forgive you. But if you do not forgive others, then your Father will not forgive your transgressions."

Ephesians 4:32 (ICB) - "Be kind and loving to each other. Forgive each other just as God forgave you in Christ.

Luke 17:3-4 (ICB) - "So be careful! If your brother sins, tell him he is wrong. But if he is sorry and stops sinning, forgive him. If your brother sins against you seven times in one day, but he says that he is sorry each time, then forgive him."

Family commitment: Today I will intentionally...

Family Declaration:

Together, let's declare: "We choose to foster forgiveness in our relationships, releasing resentment and extending grace and reconciliation to those who have wronged us. May our forgiveness bring healing and restoration, reflecting the love of Christ in our family and community."

Thanksgiving and Prayer for Guidance:

Heavenly Father, we come before you, acknowledging our need for forgiveness and reconciliation in our relationships. Thank You, Heavenly Father, for the gift of forgiveness demonstrated through Christ's sacrificial love. Help us to cultivate a heart of forgiveness, choosing to release resentment and grudges and extend grace and reconciliation to those who have wronged us, just as You have forgiven us. May our forgiveness bring healing and restoration, reflecting the love of Christ in our family and in our community." In Jesus' name, we pray. Amen.

Day 22: Cultivating Gratitude

Welcome to Day 22 of our family devotional journey! Today, we revisit the virtue of gratitude and re-explore the transformative practice of gratitude. Let's dive deeper into its profound impact on our hearts and perspectives. Let's delve into how we can practically apply this truth to our lives.

Scripture: 1 Thessalonians 5:18

"In everything give thanks; for this is God's will for you in Christ Jesus." (NASB)

'And in the midst of everything be always giving thanks, for this is God's perfect plan for you in Christ Jesus. '(TPT)

"Give thanks whatever happens. That is what God wants for you in Christ Jesus." (ICB)

Envisioning a Practical Connection:

Imagine a family where gratitude abounds, where every day is marked by thankfulness for the blessings, big and small, that surround them. As adults, this means cultivating a heart of gratitude, choosing to see the goodness of God in every circumstance. For children, tweens, and teens, it's about learning to recognize and appreciate the blessings in their lives, fostering a spirit of thankfulness in all they do.

Clarifying the Teaching:

This scripture reminds us of the importance of gratitude in our daily lives. It urges us to shift from complaint and dissatisfaction to a posture of happiness, satisfaction, thanksgiving and praise. As a family, let's embrace the practice of cultivating gratitude, knowing that it leads to joy, contentment, and a deeper appreciation for God's goodness.

Benefits of Cultivating Gratitude:

Cultivating gratitude leads to joy, contentment, and a deeper appreciation for God's blessings. It shifts our focus from what we lack to what we have, fostering a spirit of abundance and generosity. When we take time to really acknowledge and thank God for the daily blessings that are often overlooked and are often taken for granted such as being alive, breathing and being able to eat, think and move, we become more aware of all the goodness, and the provisions that go beyond material things which are the divine blessings we receive daily. Let's embrace the blessings that come from cultivating gratitude, knowing that it brings glory to God and transforms our hearts and perspectives.

Family Reflection: Share about new experiences both positive and challenging. Use this time to discuss things seen, heard or situations you or others are presently facing that relate to the virtue of Gratitude.

Adult Perspective: Reflect on moments when gratitude brought joy and contentment to your life. How can you cultivate a spirit of gratitude in your daily routine, choosing to give thanks in all circumstances, knowing that God's goodness surrounds you?

Child Perspective: Think about something you're grateful for today. How does it make you feel, and how can you practice gratitude by expressing thanks to God and others for the blessings in your life?

Tween Perspective: Consider the importance of gratitude in fostering joy and contentment. How can you cultivate a spirit of thankfulness in your daily routine, choosing to see the goodness of God in every circumstance?

Teen Perspective: Reflect on the impact of gratitude on your perspective and attitude. How can you be intentional about cultivating gratitude, choosing to give thanks in all circumstances, knowing that God's blessings abound?

Transforming Our Mind:

Think about practical ways to cultivate gratitude in your family and community. How can you prioritize thanksgiving and praise in your daily routine, choosing to see the goodness of God in every circumstance, and expressing gratitude to Him and others for the blessings in your life?

Additional Reading:

Explore these scriptures related to the theme. Read out loud, then share your thoughts about what the scriptures are saying and teaching us, especially about God, Christ Jesus and who we are as children of God:

Colossians 3:15 (ICB) - "Let the peace that Christ gives control your thinking. You were all called together in one body to have peace. Always be thankful."

1 Thessalonians 5:18 "Give thanks whatever happens. That is what God wants for you in Christ Jesus." (ICB)

Psalms 95:2 (TPT) - "Everyone come meet his face with a thankful heart. Don't hold back your praises; make him great by your shouts of joy!

Colossians 2:6-7 (NASB) - "having been firmly rooted and now being built up in Him and established in your faith, just as you were instructed, and overflowing with gratitude. Therefore as you have received Christ Jesus the Lord, so walk in Him, '

Psalms 118:24 (NASB) - 'This is the day which the Lord has made; Let's rejoice and be glad in it.

Family commitment: Today I will intentionally...

Family Declaration:

Together, let's declare: "We choose to cultivate gratitude in our daily lives, giving thanks in all circumstances and acknowledging God's goodness and blessings. May our gratitude bring joy, contentment, and a deeper appreciation for His love and provision in our family and community."

Thanksgiving and Prayer for Guidance:

Thank You, Heavenly Father, for the gift of Your goodness and blessings in our lives. Heavenly Father, we come before you with grateful hearts, acknowledging Your goodness and blessings in our lives. Help us to cultivate a spirit of gratitude, choosing to give thanks in all circumstances, knowing that Your love and provision surround us. May our gratitude bring joy, contentment, and a deeper appreciation for Your love and provision in our family and community." In Jesus' name, we pray. Amen.

Day 23: Nurturing Compassion

Welcome to Day 23 of our family devotional journey! Today, we explore the transformative power of compassion and its profound impact on our relationships, attitudes and those around us. Let's delve into how we can practically apply this truth and virtue in our lives.

Scripture: Colossians 3:12

"So, as those who have been chosen of God, holy and beloved, put on a heart of compassion, kindness, humility, gentleness, and patience." (NASB)

'You are always and dearly loved by God! So robe yourself with virtues of God , since you have been divinely chosen to be holy. Be merciful as you endeavor to understand others, and be compassionate, showing kindness toward all. Be gentle and humble, unoffendable in your patience with others.' (TPT)

"God has chosen you and made you his holy people. He loves you. So always do these things: Show mercy to others; be kind, humble, gentle, and patient." (ICB)

Envisioning a Practical Connection:

Imagine a family where compassion flows freely, where each member extends kindness and understanding to one another and those in need. As adults, this means cultivating a heart of compassion, choosing to empathize with the struggles and challenges of others. For children, tweens, and teens, it's about learning to see beyond themselves, showing empathy and kindness to those who are hurting or marginalized, meaning those who are treated as insignificant, unimportant, worthless, irrelevant to life, unvalued and unwanted outsiders who don't deserve consideration.

Clarifying the Teaching:

This scripture reminds us of the importance of compassion in our interactions with others. It urges us to shift from self-centeredness to a posture of empathy and kindness. As a family, let's embrace the practice of nurturing compassion, knowing that it brings healing, comfort, and hope to those in need. Compassion provides care and love to those who are sad and not feeling loved or liked. This is especially true for those who do not feel confident in who they are yet or unsafe in sharing their hurt or needs.

Benefits of Nurturing Compassion:

Nurturing compassion leads to empathy, kindness, and a deeper connection with others. It fosters unity and understanding within our families and our communities, breaking down barriers and building bridges of love, support and belonging. Cultivating compassion invites the culture of God's Kingdom to change and break the continuation of being criticized, being made fun of for our unique differences or for what we need, whether it's material things or emotional needs. Compassion and empathy towards each other builds that sense of safety, being seen, cared about and feeling safe about sharing how we feel and what we need. Many times, people suffer in silence, holding their needs and pains to themselves. Let's embrace the blessings that come from nurturing compassion, knowing that it heals broken hearts, supports those who may be struggling with something, reflects the heart of Christ and brings glory to God.

Family Reflection:

Adult Perspective: Reflect on moments when compassion made a difference in your relationships. How can you cultivate a heart of compassion in your interactions with others, choosing to empathize with their struggles and extend kindness and support?

Child Perspective: Think about a time when someone showed compassion to you. How did it make you feel, and how can you practice compassion by showing empathy and kindness to others who are hurting or in need?

Tween Perspective: Consider the importance of compassion in building relationships and fostering unity. How can you cultivate a heart of compassion in your interactions with peers and family members, choosing to show empathy and kindness to those around you?

Teen Perspective: Reflect on the impact of compassion in your school or community. How can you be intentional about nurturing compassion, choosing to show empathy and kindness to those who are hurting or marginalized, and making a positive difference in their lives?

Transforming Our Mind:

Think about practical ways to nurture compassion in your family and community. How can you prioritize empathy, kindness, and support, choosing to see the needs of others and extend compassion and love to those who are hurting or in need?

Additional Reading:

Explore these scriptures related to the theme. Read out loud, then share your thoughts about what the scriptures are saying and teaching us, especially about God and who we are as children of God:

Matthew 9:36 (NASB) - "Seeing the people, He felt compassion for them, because they were distressed and dispirited like sheep without a shepherd."

Luke 10:33-34 (Passion Translation) - "Then a despised Samaritan came by and saw the man, and he felt compassion for him. So he stopped, stooped over him, and gave him first aid, pouring olive oil on his wounds, disinfecting them with wine, and bandaging them to stop the bleeding."

2 Corinthians 9;12-13 (ICB) - "This service that you do helps the needs of God's people. It is also bringing more and more thanks to God. This service you do is a proof of your faith. Many people will praise God because of it. They will praise God because you follow the Good News of Christ—the gospel you say you believe. They will praise God because you freely share with them and with all others. '

Micah 6:8 (ICB) - "The Lord has told you what is good. He has told you what he wants from you: Do what is right to other people. Love being kind to others. And live humbly, trusting your God."

Family commitment: Today I will intentionally...

Family Declaration:

Together, let's declare: "We choose to nurture compassion in our relationships and interactions, showing empathy and kindness to those who are hurting or in need. May our compassion bring healing, comfort, and hope to those around us, reflecting the love of Christ in our family and community."

Thanksgiving and Prayer for Guidance: Thank You, Heavenly Father, for the gift of compassion demonstrated through Christ's sacrificial love. Heavenly Father, we come before you, asking for the grace to nurture compassion in our relationships and interactions. Help us to cultivate hearts of empathy and kindness, choosing to show empathy, kindness, compassion and love to those who are hurting or in need, just as Christ has shown compassion to us. May our compassion bring healing, comfort, and hope to those around us, reflecting the love of Christ to others, in our family and in our community." In Jesus' name, we pray. Amen.

Day 24: Pursuing Peace

Welcome to Day 24 of our family devotional journey! Today, we explore the importance of pursuing peace in our relationships and communities. Let's delve into how we can practically apply this truth to our lives.

Scripture: Matthew 5:9

"Blessed are the peacemakers, for they shall be called sons of God." *(NASB)*

"'How joyful you are when you make peace! For then you will be recognized as a true child of God. '(TPT)

'Those who work to bring peace are happy. God will call them his sons.' (ICB)

Envisioning a Practical Connection:

Imagine a family where peace reigns supreme, where conflicts are resolved with grace, love and understanding, and where love prevails and wins in every interaction. As adults, this means actively seeking peace in our relationships, choosing to extend forgiveness and pursue reconciliation. For children, tweens, and teens, it's about learning to be peacemakers in their interactions with others, seeking to resolve conflicts and build bridges of understanding.

Clarifying the Teaching:

This scripture reminds us of the importance of pursuing peace in our relationships and interactions. It urges us to shift our responses to life circumstances, conflicts and interactions from division and discord to a posture of reconciliation and unity. In today's culture, there are so many videos, actions and responses fuel tension, hostility, and violence. As a family, let's embrace the practice of pursuing peace, knowing that it fosters harmony, understanding, and love in our relationships and communities.

Benefits of Pursuing Peace:

Pursuing peace leads to reconciliation, unity, and a deeper sense of connection with others. It fosters understanding and empathy, breaking down barriers and building bridges of reconciliation. Seek ways to establish peace and be at peace. Let's embrace the blessings that come from pursuing peace, knowing that it reflects the heart of Christ and brings glory to God.

Family Reflection:

Adult Perspective: Reflect on moments when pursuing peace brought healing and reconciliation in your relationships. How can you actively seek peace in your interactions with others, choosing forgiveness and reconciliation even in the midst of conflict?

Child Perspective: Think about a time when you helped resolve a conflict between friends or siblings. How did it feel, and how can you be a peacemaker in your interactions with others, seeking to build bridges of understanding and reconciliation?

Tween Perspective: Consider the importance of pursuing peace in building strong friendships and resolving conflicts. How can you actively seek peace in your interactions with peers and family members, choosing forgiveness and reconciliation even when it's difficult?

Teen Perspective: Reflect on the impact of pursuing peace in your school or community. How can you be intentional about being a peacemaker, seeking to resolve conflicts and build bridges of understanding and reconciliation among your peers?

Transforming Our Mind:

Think about practical ways to pursue peace in your family and community. How can you prioritize forgiveness, empathy, and reconciliation in your interactions with others, choosing to be peacemakers and ambassadors of Christ's love and grace?

Additional Reading:

Explore these scriptures related to the theme. Read out loud, then share your thoughts about what the scriptures are saying and teaching us, especially about God and who we are as children of God:

> *Romans 12:18 (NASB)* - " If possible, so far as it depends on you, be at peace with all people." (NASB)

> *James 3:18 (TPT)* - "And those who are peacemakers will plant seeds of peace and reap a harvest of righteousness."

> *Proverbs 16:7 (NASB)* - "The highway of the upright is to turn away from evil; One who watches his way protects his life.."

> Proverbs 16:17 (ICB) - "A good person stays away from evil. A person who watches what he does protects his life.

> *Romans 14:19 (TPT)* - 'So then, make it your top priority to live a life of peace with harmony in your relationships, eagerly seeking to strengthen and encourage one another. '

Family commitment: Today I will intentionally...

Family Declaration:

Together, let's declare: "We choose to pursue peace in our relationships and interactions, seeking reconciliation and understanding with grace and empathy. May our pursuit of peace foster harmony, unity, and love in our family and community."

Thanksgiving and Prayer for Guidance:

Thank You, Heavenly Father, for the gift of peace demonstrated through Christ's sacrificial love. Heavenly Father, we come before you, acknowledging our need for peace in our relationships and communities. Help us to be peacemakers, actively seeking reconciliation and understanding in our interactions with others, that Your love and grace may abound. Help us pursue peace that fosters harmony, unity, and love in our family and community." In Jesus' name, we pray. Amen.

Day 25: Seeking God's Wisdom

Welcome to Day 25 of our family devotional journey! Today, we revisit and delve deeper into the essential and beneficial practice of seeking God's wisdom and understanding. Let's explore how we can practically apply this truth to our lives.

Scriptures: **Proverbs 9:10-12**

'The fear of the Lord is the beginning of wisdom, And the knowledge of the Holy One is understanding. For by me your days will be multiplied, And years of life will be added to you. If you are wise, you are wise for yourself, And if you scoff, you alone will suffer from it. ' (NASB)

"The starting point for acquiring wisdom is to be consumed with awe as you worship Yahweh. To receive the revelation of the Holy One, you must come to the one who has living-understanding. Wisdom will extend your life, making every year more fruitful than the one before. So it is to your advantage to be wise. But to ignore the counsel of wisdom is to invite trouble into your life. ' (TPT)

"Wisdom begins with respect for the Lord. And understanding begins with knowing God, the Holy One. If you live wisely, you will live a long time. Wisdom will add years to your life. The wise person is rewarded by his wisdom. But a person who makes fun of wisdom will suffer for it.' (ICB)

Envisioning a Practical Connection:

Imagine a family where seeking God's wisdom is a foundational practice, where decisions are made with divine guidance and understanding. As adults, this means prioritizing your prayer life, engaging in intentional moments to fellowship with God and learn God. It means to take time to study his word, to learn his vastness and seek God's wisdom in every aspect of our lives, trusting in His guidance for direction and discernment. For children, tweens, and teens, it's about learning to turn to God in prayer, fellowship with him, hang out with him, talk with him, confiding in him as a father and friend, seeking His wisdom and understanding in your experiences, decisions and challenges.

Clarifying the Teaching:

This scripture reminds us that seeking God for who he is, and not for what we can get from him, is the beginning of wisdom in our lives. It reveals the connection between our deep respect for God, not wanting to displease or dishonor him, as the beginning to gaining wisdom. Understanding comes from truly learning God and knowing God, seeing God properly for who he is, as our loving, guiding, compassionate, caring Father. Wisdom is gained through our intentional fellowship in learning God through his word, getting to know God through fellowshipping with God, confiding in God and being open to asking for wisdom while believing and trusting him to provide exactly what we need.

Wisdom is God's way of doing and seeing things, insight to apply in our lives for our good. Our respect for HIM, knowledge of him and our intimate connection in fellowship with God is directly linked to knowing him and understanding how to apply wisdom in our everyday lives. The virtue of wisdom in the scriptures we have studied and meditated enduring this journey has urged us to shift from relying solely on our understanding to trusting in God's infinite wisdom. As a family, let's embrace the practice of seeking God's wisdom, knowing that it brings clarity, direction, and discernment in all circumstances.

Benefits of Seeking God's Wisdom:

Seeking God's wisdom leads to clarity, direction, discernment in our lives and gives us advantages in our lives, including a long fruitful life. It empowers us to make decisions aligned with God's will, avoiding pitfalls and pursuing His purposes for us. Let's embrace the blessings that come from seeking God's wisdom, knowing that it leads to a life of fulfillment and fruitfulness.

Family Reflection: Share about new experiences both positive and challenging. Use this time to discuss things seen, heard or situations you or others are presently facing that relate to the virtue of wisdom.

Adult Perspective: Reflect on moments when seeking God's wisdom guided your decisions and actions. How can you cultivate a habit of seeking God's wisdom in every aspect of your life, trusting in His guidance and understanding?

Child Perspective: Think about a decision you need to make, whether it's about school, friends, or family. How can you seek God's wisdom in prayer, asking Him for guidance and understanding in your decision-making process?

Tween Perspective: Consider the importance of seeking God's wisdom in navigating challenges and uncertainties. How can you develop a habit of seeking God's wisdom in prayer, trusting in His guidance and understanding in every situation?

Teen Perspective: Reflect on the impact of seeking God's wisdom in your life. How can you be intentional about prioritizing prayer and seeking God's wisdom in decisions big and small, trusting in His guidance and understanding for your future?

Transforming Our Mind:

Think about practical ways to seek God's wisdom in your family and community. How can you prioritize prayer and seeking God's guidance in decisions and challenges, trusting in His infinite wisdom and understanding?

Additional Reading:

Explore these scriptures related to the theme. Read out loud, then share your thoughts about what the scriptures are saying and teaching us, especially about God and who we are as children of God:

Proverbs 3:5-6 (NASB) - "Trust in the Lord with all your heart and do not lean on your own understanding. In all your ways acknowledge Him, and He will make your paths straight."

Psalm 119:105 (Passion Translation) - "Truth's shining light guides me in my choices and decisions; the revelation of your word makes my pathway clear."

Proverbs 2:6 (NASB) - "For the Lord gives wisdom; from His mouth come knowledge and understanding."

James 3:17 (ICB) - "But the wisdom that comes from God is like this: First, it is pure. Then it is also peaceful, gentle, and easy to please. This wisdom is always ready to help those who are troubled and to do good for others. This wisdom is always fair and honest."

James 1:5 (ICB) -"But if any of you needs wisdom, you should ask God for it. God is generous. He enjoys giving to all people, so God will give you wisdom. But when you ask God, you must believe. Do not doubt God. Anyone who doubts is like a wave in the sea. The wind blows the wave up and down."

Proverbs 3:5-7 (TPT) -'Trust in the Lord completely, and do not rely on your own opinions. With all your heart rely on him to guide you, and he will lead you in every decision you make. Become intimate with him in whatever you do, and he will lead you wherever you go. Don't think for a moment that you know it all, for wisdom comes when you adore him with undivided devotion and avoid everything that's wrong.'

Family commitment: Today I will intentionally...

Family Declaration:

Together, let's declare: "We choose to seek God's wisdom in every aspect of our lives, trusting in His guidance and understanding for direction and discernment. May our reliance on His wisdom lead to clarity, direction, and fulfillment in our family and community."

Thanksgiving and Prayer for Guidance:

Thank You, Heavenly Father, for the gift of Your wisdom and understanding. Heavenly Father, we come before you, acknowledging our need for Your wisdom and understanding in our lives. Help us to seek Your wisdom in prayer, trusting in Your guidance, understanding, direction and discernment in every aspect of our lives and fulfillment in our family and community." In Jesus' name, we pray. Amen.

Day 26: Walking in Obedience

Welcome to Day 26 of our family devotional journey! Today, we explore the significance of walking in obedience to God's commandments and the transformative impact it has on our lives. Let's delve into how we can practically apply this truth to our daily walk with God.

Leading Scriptures: 1 John 5:3

"For this is the love of God, that we keep His commandments; and His commandments are not burdensome." (NASB)

True love for God means obeying his commands, and his commands don't weigh us down as heavy burdens. (TPT)

'Loving God means obeying his commands. And God's commands are not too hard for us. ' (ICB)

Envisioning a Practical Connection:

Imagine a family where obedience to God's commandments is not seen as a burden but as an expression of love and devotion to Him. As adults, this means aligning our actions and decisions with God's Word, recognizing His authority in our lives and choosing obedience out of love for Him. For children, tweens, and teens, it's about understanding that obedience to God brings blessings and fulfillment, and it is an act of love toward Him.

Clarifying the Teaching:

This scripture reminds us that obedience to God's commandments is an expression of our love for Him. It urges us to shift from viewing obedience as restrictive to understanding it as a pathway to blessing and intimacy with God. As a family, let's embrace the practice of walking in obedience, knowing that it leads to a life of joy, fulfillment, and closeness to God.

Benefits of Walking in Obedience:

Walking in obedience to God's commandments brings blessings, joy, and intimacy with Him. It aligns us with His will and purposes for our lives, leading to a life of fulfillment and abundance. Let's embrace the blessings that come from walking in obedience, knowing that it is an expression of our love for God and brings glory to His name.

Family Reflection:

Adult Perspective: Reflect on moments when obedience to God's commandments brought blessings and fulfillment in your life. How can you cultivate a lifestyle of obedience, aligning your actions and decisions with God's Word out of love for Him?

Child Perspective: Think about a time when you chose to obey God's commandments. How did it make you feel, and what blessings did you experience as a result? How can you continue to walk in obedience to God in your daily life?

Tween Perspective: Consider the importance of obedience in your relationship with God. How can you make obedience a priority in your actions and decisions, recognizing that it leads to blessings and closeness to God?

Teen Perspective: Reflect on the impact of obedience on your spiritual growth and maturity. How can you be intentional about walking in obedience to God's commandments, knowing that it brings blessings and fulfillment in your life?

Transforming Our Mind:

Think about practical ways to walk in obedience in your family and community. How can you prioritize aligning your actions and decisions with God's Word, recognizing His authority and choosing obedience out of love for Him?

Additional Reading:

Explore these scriptures related to the theme. Read out loud, then share your thoughts about what the scriptures are saying and teaching us, especially about God and who we are as children of God:

> *Deuteronomy 5:33 (NASB)* - "You shall walk in all the way which the Lord your God has commanded you, that you may live and that it may be well with you, and that you may prolong your days in the land which you will possess."

> *John 14:15 (TPT)* - "Loving me empowers you to obey my commands."

> *2 John 1:6 (ICB)* - *"And loving means living the way he commanded us to live. And God's command is this: that you live a life of love. You have heard this command from the beginning.'*

> *Luke 11:28 (ICB)* - 'But Jesus said, "Those who hear the teaching of God and obey it—they are the ones who are truly blessed."*

> *Psalms 119:1-2 (TPT)* - " 'You're only truly happy when you walk in total integrity, walking in the light of God's Word. What joy overwhelms everyone who keeps the ways of God, those who seek him as their heart's passion!'

Family commitment: Today I will intentionally...

Family Declaration:

Together, let's declare: "We choose to walk in obedience to God's commandments, recognizing that His ways lead to blessings and fulfillment in our lives. May our obedience be an expression of our love for Him and bring glory to His name."

Thanksgiving and Prayer for Guidance:

Heavenly Father, we come before you, acknowledging our need for Your guidance and strength to walk in obedience to Your commandments. Help us Holy Spirit to align our thoughts, actions, words and decisions with the Word of God, choosing obedience out of love for you, our heavenly father. Thank You, Heavenly Father, for the gift of Your word, Your commandments, Your insight, Your wisdom and the opportunity to walk in obedience to You.

Help us to choose to walk in obedience to Your commandments, knowing that Your ways lead to blessings and fulfillment in our lives. As we grow in knowledge, love, faith and obedience , we know that our obedience is an expression of our love for You and Christ and our obedience brings glory to Your name. We were created to glorify you. May our lives glorify you and reflect your love" In Jesus' name, we pray. Amen.

Day 27: Living in Unity

Welcome to Day 27 of our family devotional journey! Today, we explore the beauty and significance of living in unity as a family and community. Let's discover how we can practically apply this truth to our relationships and interactions.

Leading Scripture: **2 Corinthians 13:11**

'Finally, brothers and sisters, rejoice, mend your ways, be comforted, be like-minded, live in peace; and the God of love and peace will be with you. '(NASB)

'Finally, beloved friends, be cheerful! Repair whatever is broken among you, as your hearts are being knit together in perfect unity. Live continually in peace, and God, the source of love and peace, will mingle with you. ' (TPT)

'Now, brothers, I say good-bye. Live in harmony. Do what I have asked you to do. Agree with each other, and live in peace. Then the God of love and peace will be with you.' (ICB)

Envisioning a Practical Connection:

Imagine a family where unity reigns supreme and is the way of life and living, where love, harmony, and mutual respect characterize every interaction. As adults, this means fostering an environment of unity by valuing and honoring one another's differences, seeking reconciliation and understanding in times of conflict. For children, tweens, and teens, it's about learning to appreciate and celebrate the unique qualities and contributions of each family member, fostering a spirit of togetherness and cooperation.

Clarifying the Teaching:

This scripture reminds us of the beauty and goodness of living in unity with one another. It urges us to shift from division and discord to a posture of love and harmony. As a family, let's embrace the practice of living in unity, knowing that it brings joy, peace, and blessing to our relationships.

Benefits of Living in Unity:

Living in unity fosters joy, peace, and blessing in our relationships and interactions. It strengthens the bonds of love and mutual respect, creating a supportive and nurturing environment for growth and flourishing. Living in love, wisdom humility, ,forgiveness, generosity and unity is Kingdom Living. Let's embrace the blessings that come from living in unity, choosing the Kingdom of God as our way, our family, our culture and lifestyle, knowing that it glorifies God and enriches our lives.

Family Reflection:

Adult Perspective: Reflect on moments when unity brought joy and peace to your family. How can you cultivate a spirit of unity in your interactions with your family members, choosing love and harmony over division and discord?

Child Perspective: Think about a time when you felt united with your family members. How did it make you feel, and what made that experience special? How can you contribute to fostering unity in your family?

Tween Perspective: Consider the importance of unity in building strong family bonds. How can you celebrate and appreciate the unique qualities and contributions of each family member, fostering a spirit of togetherness and cooperation?

Teen Perspective: Reflect on the impact of unity on your family dynamics. How can you be intentional about fostering unity in your family, seeking reconciliation and understanding in times of conflict and division?

Transforming Our Mind:

Think about practical ways to foster unity in your family and community. How can you prioritize love, harmony, and mutual respect in your interactions, seeking reconciliation and understanding in times of conflict and division?

Additional Reading:

Explore these scriptures related to the theme. Read out loud, then share your thoughts about what the scriptures are saying and teaching us, especially about God and who we are as children of God:

> *Ephesians 4:3 (NASB)* - "Being diligent to preserve the unity of the Spirit in the bond of peace."

> *Colossians 3:14 (Passion Translation)* - "Above all, be supernaturally infused with love for one another, and live in harmony, each with others."

> *Romans 12:16 (NASB)* - "Be of the same mind toward one another; do not be haughty in mind, but associate with the lowly. Do not be wise in your own estimation."

> *Romans 12:16 (ICB)* - "Live together in peace with each other. Do not be proud, but make friends with those who seem unimportant. Do not think how smart you are."

> *Psalm 133:1 (TPT)* 'How truly wonderful and delightful it is to see brothers and sisters living together in sweet unity! '

Family commitment: Today I will intentionally...

Family Declaration:

Together, let's declare: "We choose to live in unity with one another, valuing and honoring each other's differences, and seeking reconciliation and understanding in times of conflict. May our unity bring joy, peace, and blessing to our family and community."

Thanksgiving and Prayer for Guidance:

Thank You, Heavenly Father, for the gift of unity in our family and community. Heavenly Father, we come before you, acknowledging our need for Your grace and guidance to live in unity with one another. Help us to cultivate a spirit of love, harmony, and mutual respect in our family and community, valuing and honoring each other's differences, and seeking reconciliation and understanding in times of conflict. May our unity bring joy, peace, and blessing in our family and community." In Jesus' name, we pray. Amen.

Day 28: Embracing Forgiveness

Welcome to Day 28 of our family devotional journey! Today, we delve into the transformative power of forgiveness and its profound impact on our lives and relationships. Let's explore how we can practically apply this truth to our daily walk with God and each other.

Leading Scripture: Matthew 6:14-15

" For if you forgive *other* people for their offenses, your heavenly Father will also forgive you. But if you do not forgive *other* people, then your Father will not forgive your offenses.."(NASB)

"' And when you pray , make sure you forgive the faults of others so that your Father in heaven will also forgive you. But if you withhold forgiveness from others, your Father withholds forgiveness from you." (TPT)

"Yes, if you forgive others for the things they do wrong, then your Father in heaven will also forgive you for the things you do wrong. But if you don't forgive the wrongs of others, then your Father in heaven will not forgive the wrong things you do." (ICB)

Envisioning a Practical Connection:

Imagine a family where forgiveness flows freely, where hearts are unburdened by resentment, grudges and bitterness, and relationships are marked by grace, joy, love and reconciliation. As adults, this means cultivating a heart of forgiveness, choosing to release past hurts and offenses and extend grace to those who have wronged us. For children, tweens, and teens, it's about learning to let go of hurt and bitterness, embracing forgiveness as a pathway to healing and restoration in relationships.

Clarifying the Teaching:

This scripture reminds us of the importance of forgiveness in our lives. It urges us to update our mindset, shifting from holding onto grudges and resentment to a posture of grace, mercy, love and reconciliation. As a family, let's embrace the practice of forgiveness, knowing that it leads to freedom, healing, and unity in our relationships.

Benefits of Embracing Forgiveness:

Embracing forgiveness leads to personal freedom, healing, and unity in our relationships. It releases the unhealthy burden of resentment, anger, negative thinking and bitterness, freeing us to experience peace, love, and joy in our interactions with others. Let's embrace the blessings that come from forgiving others, knowing that it reflects the heart of Christ and brings glory to God.

Family Reflection: Share about new experiences both positive and challenging. Use this time to discuss things seen, heard or situations you or others are presently facing that relates to the virtue of Forgiveness.

Adult Perspective: Reflect on moments when forgiveness brought healing and restoration in your relationships. How can you cultivate a spirit of forgiveness in your interactions with others, choosing to extend grace and reconciliation as Christ has done for us?

Child Perspective: Think about a time when you forgave someone who hurt you. How did it feel, and how can you practice forgiveness by choosing to let go of hurt and extend grace to others?

Tween Perspective: Consider the importance of forgiveness in resolving conflicts and restoring friendships. How can you cultivate a heart of forgiveness in your interactions with peers and family members, seeking reconciliation and healing in relationships?

Teen Perspective: Reflect on the impact of forgiveness in your school or community. How can you be intentional about embracing forgiveness, choosing to release resentment and bitterness and extend grace and reconciliation to those who have wronged you?

Transforming Our Mind:

Think about practical ways to embrace forgiveness in your family and community. How can you prioritize addressing and settling grievances, wrong doings and conflicts with empathy, grace and love to find a solution, reconciliation and healing in relationships, and extending forgiveness as Christ has done for us?

Additional Reading:

Explore these scriptures related to the theme. Read out loud, then share your thoughts about what the scriptures are saying and teaching us, especially about God, Jesus Christ and who we are as children of God:

> *Colossians 1:13 -14 (NASB)* - ' ' For He rescued us from the domain of darkness, and transferred us to the kingdom of His beloved Son, in whom we have redemption, the forgiveness of sins. '

> Ephesians 1:7-8 (TPT) - 'Since we are now joined to Christ, we have been given the treasures of redemption by his blood—the total cancellation of our sins—all because of the cascading riches of his grace. This superabundant grace is already powerfully working in us, releasing all forms of wisdom and practical understanding.

> Mark 11:25-26 (TPT) - 'And whenever you stand praying, if you find that you carry something in your heart against another person, release him and forgive him so that your Father in heaven will also release you and forgive you of your faults. But if you will not release forgiveness, don't expect your Father in heaven to release you from your misdeeds."

Family Declaration:

Together, let's declare: "We choose to embrace forgiveness in our relationships, releasing resentment and extending grace and reconciliation to those who have wronged us. May our forgiveness bring healing and restoration, reflecting the love of Christ in our family and community."

Thanksgiving and Prayer for Guidance:

Thank You, Heavenly Father, for the gift of forgiveness demonstrated through Christ's sacrificial love. Heavenly Father, we come before you, acknowledging our need for forgiveness and reconciliation in our relationships. Help us to cultivate a heart of forgiveness, choosing to release irritation, grudges, resentment and extend grace to those who have wronged us, just as You have forgiven us. May forgiveness bring healing and reflect the love of Christ and Your love for us as Your children everywhere we go. May our forgiveness bring healing in our family relationships and community." In Jesus' name, we pray. Amen.

Day 29: Cultivating Generosity

Welcome to Day 29 of our family devotional journey! Today, we explore the transformative practice of cultivating generosity and its profound impact on our lives and communities. Let's discover how we can practically apply this truth to our daily walk with God and others.

Leading Scripture: 2 Corinthians 9:6-7

"Now this I say, he who sows sparingly will also reap sparingly, and he who sows bountifully will also reap bountifully. Each one must do just as he has purposed in his heart, not grudgingly or under compulsion, for God loves a cheerful giver." (NASB)

'Here's my point. A stingy sower will reap a meager harvest, but the one who sows from a generous spirit will reap an abundant harvest. Let giving flow from your heart, not from a sense of religious duty. Let it spring up freely from the joy of giving—all because God loves hilarious generosity! ' (TPT)

"Remember this: The person who plants a little will have a small harvest. But the person who plants a lot will have a big harvest. Each one should give, then, what he has decided in his heart to give. He should not give if it makes him sad. And he should not give if he thinks he is forced to give. God loves the person who gives happily." (ICB)

Envisioning a Practical Connection:

Imagine a family where generosity flows freely, where hearts are open to give and bless others abundantly. As adults, this means recognizing our blessings and purposefully sharing them with those in need, whether it's through our time, resources, or talents. For children, tweens, and teens, it's about learning the joy of giving and serving others, understanding that generosity not only blesses others but also brings fulfillment and joy to our own lives.

Clarifying the Teaching:

This scripture reminds us of the importance of cultivating a generous heart. It urges us to update our mindset, shifting from a scarcity mentality to an abundance mindset, knowing that God blesses those who give cheerfully and generously. As a family, let's embrace the practice of cultivating generosity, knowing that it brings blessings not only to others but also to ourselves.

Benefits of Cultivating Generosity:

Cultivating generosity brings blessings, joy, and fulfillment in our lives and communities. It aligns us with God's heart for giving and blesses both the giver and the receiver. Let's embrace the blessings that come from cultivating generosity, knowing that it reflects God's love and brings glory to His name.

Family Reflection:

Adult Perspective: Reflect on moments when generosity brought joy and fulfillment in your life. How can you cultivate a spirit of generosity in your family, intentionally looking for opportunities to bless others with your time, resources, and talents?

Child Perspective: Think about a time when you gave something to someone in need. How did it make you feel, and how can you continue to cultivate a heart of generosity by sharing your blessings with others?

Tween Perspective: Consider the importance of generosity in making a positive impact on your community. How can you cultivate a spirit of generosity by serving others and sharing your blessings with those in need?

Teen Perspective: Reflect on the impact of generosity on your relationships and community. How can you be intentional about cultivating generosity, looking for opportunities to bless others with your time, resources, and talents, and bringing joy and fulfillment to those around you?

Transforming Our Mind:

Think about practical ways to cultivate generosity in your family and community. How can you prioritize sharing your blessings with others, whether it's through acts of kindness, giving financially, or serving those in need, and reflect God's love through your generosity?

Additional Reading:

Explore these scriptures related to the theme. Read out loud, then share your thoughts about what the scriptures are saying and teaching us, especially about God and who we are as children of God:

Proverbs 11:25 (NASB) - "The generous person will be prosperous, and one who waters will himself be watered."

Acts 20:35 (NASB) - "In everything I showed you that by working hard in this manner you must help the weak and remember the words of the Lord Jesus, that He Himself said, 'It is more blessed to give than to receive.'"

Luke 6:38 (Passion Translation) - "Give generously and generous gifts will be given back to you, shaken down to make room for more. Abundant gifts will pour out upon you with such an overflowing measure that it will run over the top! Your measurement of generosity becomes the measurement of your return."

Luke 6:38 (ICB) - "Give, and you will receive. You will be given much. It will be poured into your hands—more than you can hold. You will be given so much that it will spill into your lap. The way you give to others is the way God will give to you."

Family commitment: Today I will intentionally...

Family Declaration:

Together, let's declare: "We choose to cultivate a spirit of generosity in our family, intentionally looking for opportunities to bless others with our time, resources, and talents. May our generosity bring joy, fulfillment, and blessings to those around us, reflecting God's love and goodness."

Thanksgiving and Prayer for Guidance:

Thank You, Heavenly Father, for the gift of generosity demonstrated through Christ's sacrificial love. Heavenly Father, we come before you, acknowledging our need for Your guidance to cultivate a spirit of generosity in our lives. Help us to recognize our blessings and purposefully share them with others, reflecting Your love and generosity to the world around us. Help us cultivate a spirit of generosity in our hearts, intentionally looking for opportunities to bless others with our time, resources, and talents. May our generosity bring joy, fulfillment, and blessings to those around us, reflecting Your love and goodness." In Jesus' name, we pray. Amen.

Day 30: Reflecting God's Love

Welcome to Day 30, the final day of our family devotional journey! Today, we reflect on the profound truth of God's love and how it shapes our identity as His beloved children.

Scriptures: 1 John 4:7-8

"Beloved, let us love one another, for love is from God; and everyone who loves is born of God and knows God. The one who does not love does not know God, for God is love." (NASB)

'Those who are loved by God, let his love continually pour from you to one another, because God is love. Everyone who loves is fathered by God and experiences an intimate knowledge of him. The one who doesn't love has yet to know God, for God is love. '(TPT)

'Dear friends, we should love each other, because love comes from God. The person who loves has become God's child and knows God. Whoever does not love does not know God, because God is love. '(ICB)

Envisioning a Practical Connection:

Imagine a family where love reigns supreme, where every interaction is marked by kindness, compassion, and grace. As adults, this means modeling God's love in our relationships, demonstrating forgiveness, empathy, and acceptance. For children, tweens, and teens, it's about understanding that they are deeply loved by God and reflecting His love in their interactions with others.

Clarifying the Teaching:

This scripture reminds us that God is the source of all love, and as His children, we are called to reflect His love in our lives. It urges us to update our mindset, shifting from a conditional view of love to understanding God's unconditional and limitless love for us. As a family, let's embrace the truth of God's love, knowing that it transforms our hearts and relationships.

Benefits of Reflecting God's Love:

Reflecting God's love brings healing, unity, and transformation in our lives and relationships. It fosters a sense of belonging and acceptance, creating a supportive and nurturing environment for growth and flourishing. Let's embrace the blessings that come from reflecting God's love, knowing that it draws us closer to Him and each other.

Family Reflection:

Adult Perspective: Reflect on moments when you experienced God's love in your life. How can you continue to reflect His love in your relationships, demonstrating kindness, compassion, and grace to those around you?

Child Perspective: Think about a time when you felt loved by God. How does knowing that you are deeply loved by Him impact the way you treat others? How can you reflect God's love in your interactions with your family and friends?

Tween Perspective: Consider the importance of reflecting God's love in your friendships and interactions with peers. How can you demonstrate kindness, empathy, and acceptance, knowing that you are deeply loved by God?

Teen Perspective: Reflect on the impact of God's love on your identity and relationships. How can you be intentional about reflecting His love in your words and actions, creating a culture of love and acceptance in your school or community?

Transforming Our Mind:

Think about practical ways to reflect God's love in your family and community. How can you prioritize demonstrating kindness, compassion, and grace in your interactions, knowing that you are deeply loved by God and called to reflect His love to the world around you?

Additional Reading:

Explore these scriptures related to the theme. Read out loud, then share your thoughts about what the scriptures are saying and teaching us, especially about God, Jesus Christ and who we are as children of God:

Ephesians 2:10 (NASB) - "For we are His workmanship, created in Christ Jesus for good works, which God prepared beforehand so that we would walk in them."

2 Corinthians 5:17 (Passion Translation) - "Now, if anyone is enfolded into Christ, he has become an entirely new creation. All that is related to the old order has vanished. Behold, everything is fresh and new."

Romans 8:15-16 (TPT) - "'And you did not receive the "spirit of religious duty," leading you back into the fear of never being good enough . But you have received the "Spirit of full acceptance," enfolding you into the family of God. And you will never feel orphaned, for as he rises up within us, our spirits join him in saying the words of tender affection, "Beloved Father!" For the Holy Spirit makes God's fatherhood real to us as he whispers into our innermost being, "You are God's beloved child!"'"

Family commitment: Today I will intentionally...

Family Declaration:

Together, we declare: We are citizens of God's Kingdom, members of His royal family. Rooted in Christ, we commit to representing His love, grace, and righteousness in all we do. Our lives are a testament to the Kingdom's values, and through our actions, we aim to glorify our Heavenly Father.

Thanksgiving and Prayer for Guidance:

Heavenly Father, we thank You for the gift of Your unconditional love that transforms our hearts and relationships. Help us to reflect Your love in our lives, demonstrating kindness, compassion, forgiveness and grace to those around us, and drawing others closer to You through our actions. Thank you for this opportunity to learn and grow as a family. Jesus Christ as King of Your Kingdom, we thank you for being the first of many sons and daughters, and being our example to show us the values, virtues and ways for Kingdom living, thinking and being as chosen members of your royal family.

Thank you for your word and the time you blessed us with to learn You through Your word, through revelations and sharing as a family. Thank you for your word and the truth it shares about You as our Creator and Heavenly Father. Thank you for blessing us individually and collectively as a family. Help us Holy Spirit to seek first the Kingdom of God and His righteousness, Help us to be doers of the word of God, not just hearers and knowers of scriptures. We give you glory, honor and praise for who you are, Our God, our father, the one who so loves us and chose us as his. Thank you, Jesus for your life, your obedience, your words, your ministry, the gospel of the Kingdom of God and your sacrifice. God so loved us, that he gave you so that all who believed in you would be reconciled back to God as his royal family. In Jesus' name, we pray. Amen

Our Royal 30 Day Journey Conclusion:

As we conclude our 30-day journey, let's reflect on the transformative truths we've explored together. We've learned about the importance of obedience, patience, humility, wisdom, unity, forgiveness, compassion, gratitude and generosity in our lives and relationships. Each day has been an opportunity to grow closer to God and each other as we've applied His Word to our daily lives. This is not the end, yet the beginning to growing in our knowledge, understanding and identity as a family, as God's Royal Family. This journey is one of many intentional journeys we will embark on as we seek first the Kingdom of God and his righteousness. As we seek to grow in knowledge, understanding and faith, let's keep putting into practice everything that we have learned and did to progress in your values and living Kingdom virtues. Let's continue Living Our Royalty, as Kings and Queens, the Chosen family, The Family of God where Jesus is King.

Yes, we believe !!! Now let's embrace our salvation, gained through our belief in Christ and take our place and embrace our citizenship gained through the New Covenant. Let's continue to grow in Kingdom knowledge, God's truths, faith, trust, identity, values, virtues and culture as Children of God, His Royal Family.

Next Family Intentional Journey: Learning Your Identity in Christ

As we prepare for our next 30-day family devoted time to journey deeper in God's truths and the Kingdom of God, let's focus on learning who we are in Christ. Our identity is rooted in Him, and as His beloved brothers and sisters, we are loved unconditionally, empowered by God's grace, and equipped with his Holy Spirit, gifts and talents to fulfill His purpose for our lives. Join us as we discover the richness of our identity in Christ and embrace our role as ambassadors of His Kingdom.

About the Author: Monica Renee' Griffin-Monroe

Monica's spiritual journey is a testament to the transformative power of faith and an unwavering pursuit of God's truth. Raised in a Jehovah's Witnesses household, Monica was introduced to scripture from a young age, but it wasn't until she left the Kingdom Hall at twelve and later, at nineteen, began visiting a variety of Christian churches, that she truly began to seek God for herself. This search led to a profound personal revelation and the beginning of studying God's word that led to her confession and salvation at 19 years old.

Facing life's trials, including a pivotal moment at thirty-three when her marriage ended, leaving her to raise a young son alone, Monica turned to God with renewed fervor. Her dedication to understanding God's word and aligning her life with His will transformed her approach to faith, moving beyond traditional religious practices to a heartfelt, relational Christianity. A reliance on God, a surrender to God, his will and his way.

Through VBS, Monica learned of St. Paul's Bible Church and began attending small group bible studies. Monica grew in knowledge and understanding of the word of God and experienced a true sense of belonging and being a part of an inclusive, multicultural, supportive loving family of believers and followers which grew into a deep, committed walk in alignment with Yahweh, Jehovah God, marked by subsequent baptism in 2017.

Driven by the song "Make Room" by Jonathan McReynolds in 2019, Monica's spiritual path took a new direction towards seeking God earnestly to make room for God, to move things out of the way to truly make room and open space to receive him, get to know him, see him, and understand God intimately. "Open the Eyes of My Heart Lord" rekindled this desire to truly know God, spend time with God personally and surrender again, with a refreshed commitment.

In 2020, Monica prioritized God as first priority and began devoting time daily to meet with God, talk to God, fellowship with God as a father and friend, learn God and spend intimate time with God. This was a new level of vulnerability, openness, confiding, being still to meditate and listen. This opened a new level which led to growing in love with God, knowing him, recognizing how he operates, experiencing him and hearing from him. His word came alive, embodying the love, light and wisdom of God. In 2021, dear friends Gustave & Renee Tucker welcomed her into a small group that began the journey of exponential learning, revealing and healing through a group study of " Living From The Heart That Jesus Gave You" from The Life Model.

In 2022, Monica began a new and started on a path and plan of wellbeing. Her Divine Guide on The Side, Nina Drape, MA, LCPC encouraged her to ask God what she should study in this season. Her quest for insight and knowledge led her to profound insights through the teachings of Myles Munroe, Tony Evans, and Bill Winston, highlighting a significant gap in her previous religious education—the message and centrality of the Kingdom of God, Jesus' ministry.

Her intense experience with The Life Development Center (LDC); Leading Lights Training Experience in Chicago deepened her understanding of her universal and individual purpose within the Kingdom of God. This experience revealed and clarified her calling as a child of God, Kingdom Citizen and ambassador for Christ. From that life changing experience with LDC, through the Leading Lights Training Experience, Monica has committed to taking her place in the Kingdom of God and advancing awareness of the Kingdom of God, Kingdom values, principles, and culture.

She is passionate about transformation in the areas of Education, Improving Instruction, Effectiveness, Wellbeing, Emotional Wellness, Healing, Identity, Community and Family. **Monica is L.I.T.T.** Monica is Living Intentionally to Transform & Thrive in Life.

Professionally, Monica is a seasoned educator and transformational leader in the field of education, dedicated to creating optimal learning experiences and fostering holistic development. She is the CEO of Stay LITT LLC, where she is a Consulting Servant Leader of Change Management and Advancer of Education 4.0. She provides consulting and Professional Transformation Services to build the capacity of organizations, Institutions, Instructional Leaders and facilitators. She is multifaceted in skills to optimize, build capacity, organize, transform and Improve Curriculum, Instruction, Facilitation, Learning experiences, Learning environments, Effectiveness and Wellbeing for All. Her professional endeavors mirror her spiritual mission: to inspire, empower and equip individuals to discover, develop, transform and deploy their divine gifts and identities. Monica globally supports the advancement of people discovering their divine identity, purpose and living a purpose-driven value-based intentional life.

She is committed to serving others, advancing the Kingdom of God and making a Kingdom Driven difference in the world.

Monica serves as a beacon of love, hope, positivity, light, resourcefulness and guidance, crafting resources and leading initiatives that support believers in understanding their royal identity in Christ. Her work extends beyond personal growth, aiming to cultivate communities that embody love, wellbeing, and the transformative principles and power of the Kingdom of God.

Monica is a devoted daughter, mother, disciple, writer, educator, orator, consultant, coach, and optimizer dedicated to improving instruction, learning, and information dissemination. Through Stay LITT Ministries, social media, speaking engagements, and her series of Intentional Journey Guides for believers and those seeking to grow in truth and faith, Monica has answered the call to reveal God's truths and share the good news of the Kingdom of God.

Monica shares God's word, insights, and wisdom gained along her journey, guiding others to realize the love of a loving Father, His purpose, His plan, the Appointed King, and their identity and place as God's chosen children. She inspires believers to live intentional joy-filled lives that glorify God, align with His will, purpose and plan to advance His Kingdom on Earth.

Her mission is to help others grow in faith, learn and embrace their divine identity, and increase their knowledge and understanding of the Kingdom of God. Monica encourages individuals to intentionally seek to know God, grow in relationship with God, be open to transformation, renew their minds, take their place and walk in their Divine Role as God's Children. She serves to ignite and support the realization and rejuvenation that we are fearfully and wonderfully made and designed by God with divine purpose, gifts, and potential to align with the plans he has for believers individually and collectively, to take our place, shine his light and make a Kingdom driven difference in our world.

~ A Personal Message From The Author ~

Turn The Page

From the Author:

As I embrace my identity, transformation and calling, I will embrace and honor my God given name. The name that will never change. The name that describes me and the daughter God created and purposed me to be.

As I have journeyed in life, my name has grown and changed. It speaks to my journey, it carries stories, it carries the past, my experiences, lessons, first of many, the best gift, my Merciful Gift of God, the process of equipping me, the healing and preparation for my journey ahead. Monica Renee' Griffin-Monroe, Yes... That is my legal name. A name that tells my story.

Yet, as I am moving with the seasons of my life, I have been blessed with a new life, a new beginning, a found purpose, a Kingdom driven mission, a new me and a new way of living and loving. I am in the second half of my life, the best half and I have decided that I will affectionately go by my God Given birth name, Monica Renee'.

There is so much significance in my name... Today I step into my new life, today I take my place in God's Kingdom, embracing the new me... Loving her immensely. Yahweh is my Heavenly Father. I embrace my adoption. I am my Father's Beloved Daughter.

I am Daddy's Gurl, I am Monica Renee'.

Sharing HIS Love, Shining HIS Light & Being HIS Salt

Love, Light & Salt

Stay **LITT** LLC
Stay Living Intentionally To
Transform & Thrive

For more information, contact Monica Renee'. Explore and learn about Stay LITT as we grow and Stay L.I.T.T. in Life (Stay Living Intentionally to Transform & Thrive)

- Email: staylittministries@gmail.com
- Social Media:
    - TikTok @choosingthekingdom
    - Instagram: @Staylittllc
- Stay LITT Soul Care Essentials www.staylitt.shop
    - Emotional Wellness Luxe Candles
    - Emotional Wellness Luxe Sprays
    - & More
- Stay LITT Ministries www.staylittsoulcare.com
    - Stay LITT Safe Sircle Book Journey
    - Stay LITT Safe Sircle Socials, Retreats, Events & Vacations
- Stay LITT LLC ~Education Transformation Solutions
    - Instructional Consulting Services
        - We are L.I.T.T. We are Leveraging Innovation to Transform & Thrive in Educational Systems, regardless of Setting, including Home Schooling.
        - We Enhance Facilitation, Collaborative Team Teaching and IEP Implementation.
        - We are Accommodations, Differentiation and Personalized Learning Experts.
        - We design solutions to organize, optimize and manage learning for ALL.
    - www.staylittllc.com
    - monica@staylittllc.com